NOTTINGHAM

A HISTORY

JILL ARMITAGE

AMBERLEY

First published 2015

Amberley Publishing
The Hill, Stroud
Gloucestershire, GL5 4EP

www.amberley-books.com

Copyright © Jill Armitage, 2015

ISBN 978 1 4456 3498 2 (print)
ISBN 978 1 4456 3519 4 (ebook)

British Library Cataloguing in Publication Data.
A catalogue record for this book is available from
the British Library.

Typesetting by Amberley Publishing.
Printed in the UK.

CONTENTS

Acknowledgements   4

1   Roman Nottingham   5

2   The Normans Arrive   12

3   Nottingham in the Twelfth Century   18

4   Robin Hood – Nottingham's Hero   23

5   Churches and Charities   27

6   Trade in the Middle Ages   36

7   Nottingham Castle   41

8   Nottingham in the Seventeenth Century   48

9   Caves   55

10 The Town of Cave Dwellings   63

11 Nottingham in the Eighteenth Century   71

12 The Hosiery and Lace Trade   79

13 Crime and Punishment   86

14 Nottingham's Major Industries in the Nineteenth
    and Twentieth Centuries   95

15 Transport   108

16 Nottingham in the Twentieth Century   116

17 Famous Nottingham Characters   122

ACKNOWLEDGEMENTS

I would like to thank all who have shared ideas, made suggestions and given information to make this book possible. My most grateful thanks go to the individuals, organizations and libraries whose old photographs I was able to copy for inclusion. Some of the period illustrations have come from obscure sources, making it difficult to credit the originators or the people who have preserved the images. To them all I give my sincere thanks.

1

ROMAN NOTTINGHAM

Nottingham's early history is very sparse. Many towns can trace their roots to pre-Roman days, but the evidence of any Roman and pre-Roman settlement is very limited in and around the city of Nottingham, despite the fact that the Roman Army built a few garrisons and roads running through Nottinghamshire. The present A46 was the Roman Fosse Way. The road from Littleborough to Bawtry and the road from Derby to Long Eaton were routes laid out by Roman road surveyors. Evidence of Roman settlements have been seen in the Trent Valley and in the north and west of the county, but Nottingham centre seems to have been bypassed by the Romans.

According to *History & Antiquities of Nottingham* by James Orange, Nottingham was affected very little by the Romans but continued to be inhabited by the Celtic Coritanian (meaning woodland) tribe. The Coritanians stood next in power, rank and strength to their neighbours the Brigante tribe who occupied all the northern counties of England. The Celtic tribes people lived in hillforts, built, as the name implies, on dominant hilltops. From scant early records, it is possible that they inhabited what we now know as castle hill. With cliffs 130 feet (40 m) high to the south and west, the site holds a very commanding position. Their place for divine worship where the Druids offered their sacrifices could have been Baalim Hill (Malin Hill), a sacred enclosure now the site of St Mary's church. Malin Hill is an ancient bridle path from the old town surrounding St Mary's church – the English borough – down to the Meadows, probably the oldest route out of Nottingham to the south-east, although without any written proof this is all conjecture.

Under the command of Suetonius Paulinus, the Romans conquered the natives and published a decree abolishing their rites and ceremonies. James Orange states that the Romans built a fort at Holly Hill near Arnold. One of his contemporaries, Dr Gale, expresses the opinion that the Roman station Causennis occupied Nottingham centre, using the caves and subterranean chambers as granaries to store grain. We are working on the very edge of history, and the only thing we can be sure of is that nearly every record relating to Nottingham during this period has perished.

But that's not to say Nottingham is without any Roman relics. In 1937, an area of woodland less than 3 miles north-west of the city centre was scheduled for council housing and was to become the Broxtowe estate. While the planners concentrated on its street patterns designed in elegant symmetrical ovals and halfmoons, Thoroton

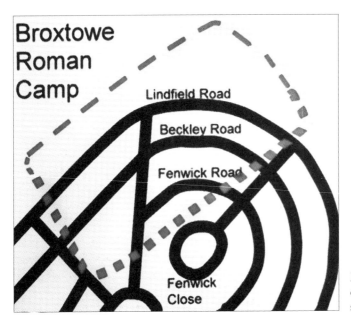

Map of the Roman fort overlaying the present street plan.

Excavating Section were felling trees to clear the woodland. While the infrastructure was being laid for drains and services in November and December 1937, a ditch and parapet 600 feet (182 m) long came to light. The outline and interior detail of what appeared to be a Roman fort appeared after further excavations. Its southern long edge was just south of the line of what was to become Fenwick Close. Its entrance was at the junction of Alwyn Road and Denton Gardens.

A drawing of the camp, bordered at the northern end by 'natural fortifications' and formed by an incline dropping 95 feet (29 m) to a valley was made by the director of excavations, George Campion – a passionate but amateur archaeologist. The distinctive 'playing card shape' is a characteristic of all Roman forts. As work continued into 1938, boys of the HM Borstal Institute at Maythorpe were loaned to help with the digging. In all, twenty boys a day worked for six weeks and moved 600 tons of earth. What was described as a large hut was found in the area that was to become Lindbridge Road. The finds were amazing. They included an ivory gaming dice and a large amount of fragmented pottery, including two parts of a quern for milling corn. There were numerous coins; the latest dated to the reign of Vespasian was struck in AD 71. Metal objects included more than thirty brooches, sickles, several iron and bronze pieces including knives and razors, and an impressive bronze skillet stamped with the name Albanvs. The finds are now on show in the University of Nottingham Museum.

The Nottingham Journal, on 15 February 1938, ran a headline announcing 'Striking Roman Finds' on the Broxtowe estate, and listed the many fascinating artefacts found in the fort. So why, despite all this, did the corporation continue to build the housing estate? The Roman fort and any further finds were reburied under tons of bricks and concrete.

The Middle Ages

Roman troops were withdrawn from Britain between AD 370–400 and the country was divided with independent Brythonic kingdoms emerging. Many of them tried to follow the Roman and Christian way of life, but trade was disrupted by war and Roman towns and villas fell into disrepair. The thousand years between the fall of Rome and the start of modern European history are known as the Middle Ages.

The Angles, Saxons, Frisians and Jutes invaded from across the North Sea and seized the land. They carved out new kingdoms for themselves in the ruins of the Roman Empire, and by AD 550 the Anglo-Saxons controlled large areas of eastern and southern Britain, while the Britons still ruled in the west and much of the north. The Nottinghamshire area was briefly covered by the kingdom of Elmet from late fifth century to the beginning of the seventh century. Conflict would last hundreds of years.

Anglo-Saxon Kingdoms included Northumbria and Mercia, the largest kingdom occupying the English Midlands. In Anglo-Saxon *mercia* means woodland kingdom and agrees closely with the name of Coritanian tribe – signifying woodland men or foresters.

The Saxons marauders, whose name is derived from the word *Seax* (a short sword that they carried) were Mercians, although for a time the Northumbrians seem to have established hegemony as far south as the Trent.

Without any earlier evidence, it would be correct to assume that the ground now occupied by Nottingham city centre seems to have been founded by the Saxons. When the Anglo-Saxon chieftain Snot settled in the area he named it Snotenceham or Snottingham. *Inga* meant 'the people of' and *ham* meant 'homestead', so Snottingham meant the homestead of Snot's people. The area east of the city, also settled by Saxons, was called Snottington. *Ton* meant farmstead or settlement and was in the area where the historic Lace Market in the City can now be found.

Coinage

Slaves and cattle were the first type of money before metal was used, and many of the ancient coins were stamped with a beast. The Saxons introduced coinage and the silver penny was introduced in the reign of Offa, King of Mercia AD 757–96, and remained the accepted coin of the realm until the reign of Edward I (1272–1307) – a period of around 500 years.

There are coins and documentary evidence of the existence of the Nottingham Mint from the year 928 until 1201, but a mint must have been in existence for a long period prior to this. The chroniclers record that after the death of Alfred the Great in 899, all of England accepted his son Edward the Elder as king. A man named Osulf was a Nottingham moneyer working in the reign of Edward the Elder. In 920, Edward's coinage read 'EADVVEARD REX'. The fact that York continued to produce its own coinage suggests that Edward's authority was not accepted in Viking-ruled Northumbria.

Then, in AD 928, King Athelstan (son of Edward the Elder), Wulferhelme, Archbishop of Canterbury and all the great and powerful men of the kingdom decided that the whole coinage of the realm would be alike and bear the King's portrait. They also agreed that every town was entitled to one mint/moneyer; the great cities of London, Canterbury and Winchester had eight, seven and six, respectively. Nottingham was allowed two.

Early silver coins struck at Nottingham in the reign of Athelstan (925–40) have *Edetstah R. L. Saxorum* (King of the Saxons) on the observe, the cross pattee on each side, and on the reverse, Edelnod of Snotenceham. Edelnod was the moneyer, and Snotenceham meant minted in Nottingham. Any coin that does not bear the king's portrait was issued prior to 928 before the edict came into operation.

The Vikings

Viking raids began in England in the late eighth century. They were largely of the 'hit and run' kind, but in AD 789, the Vikings raided the southern coast of England and soon no region of the British Isles was safe. In 865, various Viking armies combined and landed in East Anglia, not to raid but to conquer the four Anglo-Saxon kingdoms of England. The annals describe them as Vikings from an old Norse word meaning 'sea raiders', but they were also known as the Great Heathen Army because their combined force came from the lands of Scandinavia – Denmark, Norway and Sweden. They collectively took the name 'Danes'.

England was again divided. In AD 874, the Danes conquered and settled in the east in East Anglia, Mercia and Northumbria, pushing the Anglo-Saxons south and west and into Wales. In AD 866, they captured the Northumbrian stronghold of *Jorvik* (York), and then the following year the army moved south and invaded the kingdom of Mercia. The Danes were provided with good steel armour, and under Ivar the Boneless and his brother Halfdan Ragnarsson, they attacked Nottingham. The Danish warriors had a weapon unknown to the Saxons – the bow and arrow. An indispensable qualification of every Danish warrior was to shoot well with a bow, and soon the Saxons were dying in their hundreds from the arrows without being able to get close enough to their enemies to strike a blow. Camden, who lived in the days of Queen Elizabeth, wrote that the Danes 'munimented' themselves in a strong tower erected on an exceedingly steep rock. That would signify that there was a strong tower and some form of fortress erected on the later castle site by the Saxons before the Danish invasion.

The Danes captured the town of Nottingham in AD 868 and subsequently set up their winter quarters there. The Mercian king, Burghred, responded by allying with King Aethelred of Wessex, and with a combined force, they laid siege to the town. Although the Anglo-Saxons were unable to recapture Nottingham, a truce was agreed whereby the Danes withdrew to Jorvik (York) where they remained for over a year, gathering their strength for further assaults.

In the area that is now the East Midlands, the Danes created five fortified boroughs for five detached armies who settled the area and introduced their native laws and customs, known as Danelaw. The boroughs were Nottingham, Derby, Leicester, Lincoln and Stamford. The first four would later become county towns. Each of the five boroughs was ruled as a Danish *Jarldom*, controlling lands around a fortified *burh* or town that served as the centre of political power. The rulers were probably initially

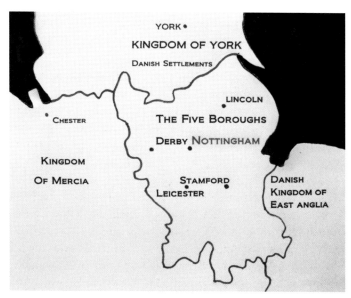

The five Danish boroughs.

subject to their overlords in the Viking Kingdom of Jorvik. They would sometimes operate their armies independently but often in alliance with neighbouring rulers. For many years, the five boroughs were a separate and well-defined area of the country where rulers sought support from its leaders.

After a brief spell at Repton, Danish reoccupation and settlement of Nottingham began in AD 877. Alfred the Great then besieged the town and took it from them. On his death in AD 899, his son Edward became king. More conflict occurred during AD 916/7 under Edward's sister, Aethelflaed of Mercia. Edward and Aethelflaed captured the East Midlands and East Anglia from the Danes in 917, and Edward became ruler of Mercia in 918 when his sister Aethelflaed died. He recovered the five boroughs and united the kingdom of Mercia with his own kingdom of Wessex. He then enclosed the whole of Nottingham with a strong wall, showing that as one of the five boroughs it was an important settlement.

All but two of his charters give his title as *Anglorum Saxonum rex* or 'king of the Anglo-Saxons'. He was the second king of the Anglo-Saxons, as this title was created by his father Alfred the Great.

Nottingham's City Wall
The wall that surrounded the town of Nottingham had a circumference that exceeded 2 miles. It was well flanked with towers and buttress and had several gates. From the castle on the hill, the wall ran in an oblique north-east direction down Butt Dyke – now Park Row to Chapel Bar.

In the 1960s, Maid Marion Way, the inner relief road, was under construction from Chapel Bar to Canal Street. It cut through some of Nottingham's oldest streets, and while excavating between Park Row and Mount Street in 1964, workmen discovered the old town wall that had formed the western boundary of the old town.

Chapel Bar was a significant location. The name 'Bar' is Scandinavian and means gate. Chapel Bar was the old west gate into the walled enclosure of Nottingham. It was given the name because built into or beside the gate was a *proseucha* – oratory or chapel for the use of travellers passing through the gate. In the days when travel was fraught with danger, they could pray here for a safe journey. The ancient gate was probably replaced around 1154 because it had ceased to give significant physical protection. Much of the wall was replaced at this time too. The twelfth-century Chapel Bar gateway, constructed during the reign of Henry II, who gave the town the first of its royal charters, survived as a picturesque ruin until 1743. It was the last remaining town gate of Nottingham. The name remains, but there is no trace of the gateway now.

Illustrations that have survived show two drum towers flanking an entrance passage that would be closed by a portcullis. Its appearance was very similar to the gateway to the castle.

From Chapel Bar, the city wall continued north-east through Roper's Close. Traces of the wall were found by workmen digging the foundations of the Shakespeare Inn and neighbouring properties. The line of the wall crossed Boot Lane (now Milton Street).

An artist's impression of Chapel Bar – the last remaining town gate in Nottingham, demolished in the eighteenth century.

There may have been a postern gate for the convenience of the inhabitants here. It was too narrow to allow carriages to pass through until it was widened in the early part of the fourteenth century.

There was another gate called Cow Gate that stood near Milton Head. Because of the name, it can be assumed that this was the way the cattle were herded into the town for market. Parts of the foundations of the city wall are still discoverable in the cellars and basements of houses standing in the middle of Parliament Row and the east side of Clumber Street.

York Street used to be the main thoroughfare where there was a north gate. The wall followed Glasshouse Street forming a curve, then down to what is now Broad Street and Carter Gate – the entrance for the carters or tradespeople. At Fisher Gate, there was a portcullis, or drawn bridge over the foss or ditch, connecting the town with the opposite rock. The wall continued to Hollow Stone and Narrow Marsh, then southwards down the west side of Garner Hill. It then formed an acute angle running up Mont Lane (now Middle Hill) in a curve to the Weekday Cross, enclosing the town hall.

It continued unbroken at the back of the houses on Middle Pavement to Drury Hill, opposite the end of Bridlesmith Gate where there was a postern or mall gate. Here there was a gatehouse, which was converted into a public house known as the Postern Gate. Under the tap room could be seen a portion of the old town wall that was 8 feet 6 inches high, 4 feet 6 inches thick and 18 feet long. Trace the wall down Low Pavement to Lister Gate, where there was another gate in the wall opposite to Church Gate, which then continued along Castle Gate in a westerly direction to join the castle wall at Brewhouse Yard.

A Bridge Over the River Trent

In AD 924, at the same time that Edward was building the wall for the benefit and security of the town, he also erected a bridge over the River Trent composed of stone piers with platforms of wood. It was probably not the first bridge to span the Trent in order to unite the northern and southern parts of the kingdom. The Romans would have found a bridge both convenient and necessary. The fact that the remains of an old Roman road has been found running from the direction of the river, crossing The Park, over the forest and on towards Arnold, might add weight to this theory. So did Edward build on the same site? A bridge would undoubtedly increase the wealth and importance of any town, and Edward's bridge would have been in use until it was superseded in 1156 by another bridge.

The five boroughs of Lincoln, Stamford, Derby, Leicester and Nottingham were five places of considerable strength in the heart of the kingdom. Following Danish conquest in 1016, Earl Sired succeeded to the newly created Earldom of the five boroughs under King Canute in 1019. By 1035, the Earldom had been subsumed into that of Leofric Earl of Mercia, and it was to form a formal administrative unit long into the future.

2

THE NORMANS ARRIVE

In 1067, the year after the Battle of Hastings, William the Conqueror captured the town of Warwick then marched north to Nottingham. As he had done at Warwick, he secured his possession of Nottingham by ordering a castle to be built there. William the Conqueror was a tyrant rather than a conqueror. Not a single Saxon lord was allowed to retain his patrimonial inheritance. William Peveril, the illegitimate son of William the Conqueror and Maud, daughter of a Saxon nobleman Ingelric, Earl of Essex, was given 162 confiscated English estates extending over a great part of the counties of Nottinghamshire and Derbyshire. Maud later married Ranulph Peveril of Hatfield Peveril, Essex, and William adopted the surname of the family his mother had married into.

Artist impression of Nottingham Castle.

Before the Norman Conquest, there was undoubtedly a tower and some form of fortress standing on the natural promontory known as Castle Rock, but any fortification would have been in keeping with Anglo-Saxon architectural tradition – smaller and far less elaborate in design to any Norman structure. In the first rush of Norman castle building there wouldn't have been time to build in stone, but the Saxons had to be subjugated to Norman power and dominance quickly. The castle on the hill was a vantage point that needed a strong tower, but it also had a symbolic function. It declared its owners power and status. In addition to holding a garrison, the castle was an administrative centre and Peveril's main residence when he wasn't engaged in the tumults of war. The first Norman castle would have been a wooden structure and of a motte-and-bailey design. When the fortress was completed, Peveril had the course of the River Leen turned to pass by his castle. The whole of the drudgery of this work was undoubtedly performed by the subdued English.

In Nottingham, William Peveril was given fifty statute acres for a garden – believed to include The Park, extending from Lenton in the west, down to the Leen and as far east as Carrington Street. The English were not only deprived of their property, houses and lands, but the means of a precarious subsistence was also taken from them by the remorseless Normans. The burgesses were prohibited from fishing in the waters of the Trent and the fishing rights were given to the monks of Lenton Priory.

Burgesses were forbidden to inhabit any houses they had on the western side of the town. A line of separation was drawn north to south commencing at Mansfield Road along Clumber Street, High Street, Bridlesmith Gate to Drury Hill (now the Broadmarsh shopping centre). No Saxon could pass over this line and from this time the town was divided into two distinct settlements. The Normans located themselves on the west of the line where a new Nottingham sprang up around Peveril's Castle. This was called the French borough, supporting the Normans in the castle.

Bottle Lane was an ancient street that led from the Norman borough to the Anglo-Saxon settlement situated on the hill to the east of the town. This was Snot's settlement in the area and where the historic Lace Market in the City can now be found. The Anglo-Saxon settlement developed into the English borough of Nottingham, defended by fortifications and clustering round the top of St Mary's Hill. It had its own church, which stood where St Mary's is now erected, its own Moot Hall (or public hall), which stood on a site on the south-east of Weekday Cross. This disappeared when the course of the L&NE Railway was altered – around 1900. Although together, the two boroughs formed the Norman Nottingham, each was ruled by its own officers and laws, and had separate administrations and courts until around 1300.

Weekday Cross

Weekday Cross was the marketplace where our Saxon forefathers met to do their marketing and conduct what passed for commerce in the days before the Norman Conquest. When Nottingham was divided, each of the two boroughs had a separate market place and Weekday Cross was the civic centre of medieval Nottingham. National and local proclamations were made at the cross. On 'Mayor-making Day'

(29 September) after a ceremony at St Mary's church, the company proceeded to the Weekday Cross from where the town clerk proclaimed the mayor and the two sheriffs of the town.

The name 'cross' is significant. The cross has been employed in every sacred ritual, designed to excite sentiments of piety, compassion and reverence. Stone crosses, originally placed by the way-side, had a double meaning. Often referred to as preaching crosses, they were where itinerate priests and monks would sermonize when in the area. On the high road, the cross was frequently placed to deter highwaymen and restrain other predators in the same way that in Market Place, the market cross was a sign of upright intentions and fair dealings.

The cost of a cross made in stone by John Mychell may not be the earliest cross erected on the site. The 1529/30 Chamberlain's Accounts itemised the cost:

Item payde for ij lod (es) ston that was okepyde (used) at the Markyt Crosse ... .xxd.
Item payde to John Mychyll for wyrkng the sam' ston ... xd.
Item payde for lyme and sande ... ijd.

There's mention of the cross at Weekday Cross in 1549 when it was positioned in the north-west of the market area. When public flagellation was a regular mode of punishment for both males and females, the Weekday Cross was frequently a starting place, owing to its close proximity to the police court at the Guild Hall. Male and female offenders who were the victims of this brutal mode of punishment were stripped to the waist and tied to the tail of a cart. The cart would be driven off and the offender whipped continuously as it made its way through the town. A young woman stealing at a draper's shop was, on market day, 12 January 1770,

fastened to a cart, and whipped all the way from the Week-day Cross to the Malt Cross, in the Market Place. Three months later, a man accused of theft was whipped in the same manner from Weekday Cross to the Malt Cross, and thence to the Hen Cross where he was liberated, a sadder and sorer man than before he started on his ignominious journey.

The degrading practice of public whipping in Nottingham was observed until 1830.

The Cross appears on the 1610 map, but many of these crosses in public places were removed and destroyed by an Act of Parliament in 1643. However, many local people often circumvented the wishes of parliament by concealing these crosses with the intention of re-erecting them when the government policy changed, which it was likely to do at short notice during the Civil War. That's what may have happened at Weekday Cross because records state that it was not removed until 1804.

The name was often changed to Weekday Market as the area continued to be the market for the English borough. Most of the commodities for this market were brought by land, but a considerable bulk was brought by water and landed at the Town Wharf by Trent Bridge. A pathway connected this wharf with the ancient market place, and Trent Bridge Footway and Sussex Street are portions of that pathway. Malin Hill is an

Welcome to Nottingham city centre

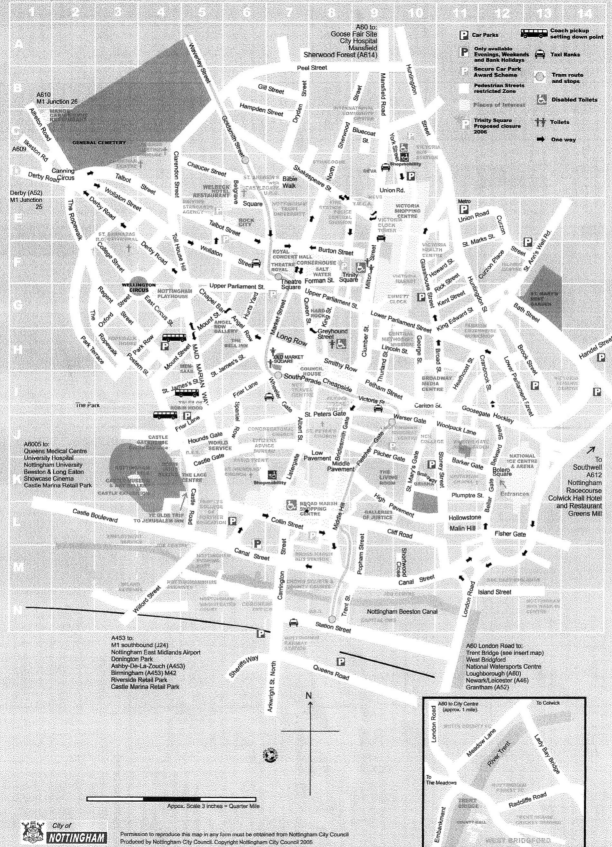

Car Parks

Only available Evenings, Weekends and Bank Holidays

Secure Car Park Award Scheme

Pedestrian Streets restricted Zone

Places of Interest

Trinity Square Proposed closure 2006

Coach pickup setting down point

Taxi Ranks

Tram route and stops

Disabled Toilets

Toilets

One way

A60 to:
Goose Fair Site
City Hospital
Mansfield
Sherwood Forest (A614)

A610
M1 Junction 26

A609

Derby (A52)
M1 Junction 25

A6005 to:
Queens Medical Centre
University Hospital
Nottingham University
Beeston & Long Eaton
Showcase Cinema
Castle Marina Retail Park

A453 to:
M1 southbound (J24)
Nottingham East Midlands Airport
Donington Park
Ashby-De-La-Zouch (A453)
Birmingham (A453) M42
Riverside Retail Park
Castle Marina Retail Park

A60 London Road to:
Trent Bridge (see insert map)
West Bridgford
National Watersports Centre
Loughborough (A60)
Newark/Leicester (A46)
Grantham (A52)

To
Southwell
A612
Nottingham
Racecourse
Colwick Hall Hotel
and Restaurant
Greens Mill

A60 to City Centre (approx. 1 mile)
To Colwick

N

Appox. Scale 3 inches = Quarter Mile

City of
NOTTINGHAM

Permission to reproduce this map in any form must be obtained from Nottingham City Council
Produced by Nottingham City Council. Copyright Nottingham City Council 2005

ancient bridle path from the old town down to the Meadows. It's probably the oldest route out of Nottingham to the south.

There is reference to the ancient market well in 1575–76 when the constables reported at the sessions that 'ye comen well at ye Weke Daye Cross be in dyecaye for want of repration'. In Market Square, the cruel amusement of bull baiting took place and, in 1541, there is mention of the bull ring being situated at the end of Fletcher Gate, which was the butchers' quarters in those days. The bull was tethered to the ring while being baited by vicious dogs – a form of popular entertainment for the masses. Slowly, the barbarous sport disappeared and was eventually banned in the late eighteenth century.

The inhabitants of the French borough established a new market, which was held on Saturdays, on what was originally the town green and is now the Old Market Square. Gradually this Saturday market became of greater importance, but Weekday Cross remained the centre of the domestic trade of Nottingham for many years after the Conquest.

Domesday Book

In the sixteenth year of his reign, William the Conqueror caused an exact survey to be taken of the lands, good and chattels of all his English subjects. It was called Domesday Book, which means 'the book of the day of judgement'. The book was completed in 1086, six years from the commencement.

The king specified that the barons, their Frenchmen and six villagers in each village had to be questioned. The barons were those who had fought with William at Hastings or followed him from Normandy shortly afterwards.

At this time, Nottingham's population would have been around 1,500. It's listed as *Notintone*, which represents the Norman pronunciation of the Anglo-Saxon place name 'Snottington'. The 'Sn' was dropped in favour of 'N', which was easier to say in the Norman tongue. The Norman pronunciation of Snottingham stuck, so we have the name Nottingham.

Norman French was the common language of masters and men. The villagers spoke but did not write vernacular English based on Anglo-Saxon. It was enriched by borrowings from every other language then known, so the commissioners wrote down the place names phonetically. The land was divided in two – the folcland or common land, and bocland – parcels of land belonging to specific people as manors or baronie.

The following is from the returns made from Nottingham, but because the castle was a royal residence it was not mentioned. However, William Peveril owned forty-eight merchant's houses in the town plus thirteen houses for his knights and eight for his husbandmen, making a total of sixty-nine houses. At this time there were 206 houses in Nottingham. Hugh, the sheriff, had thirteen, but the majority belonged to the Norman military. In the Domesday Book there are seventeen houses in the Fossata or ditch of the borough. There's mention of a watermill on the River Leen at Linton valued at 10s (50p), and another at Colwick. The River Leen, which forms a southern boundary to the town, is a 15-mile-long (24 km) tributary of the River Trent. Leen is a corruption through various interpretations of the Celtic word *llyn*, meaning lake or pool.

Later the word was changed to the Anglo-Saxon word *hlynna*, meaning streamlet. Linton is derived from Leen. Many natural features like rivers and hills had Celtic names that have been retained.

Nottinghamshire was still predominantly forest at the time of the Norman invasion. There were some existing ridgeway tracks skirting the major forest areas, but places like Sherwood Forest (the forest of the shire) remained uncharted and ill-defined. Two thirds of Nottinghamshire's villages were already established. Those place names ending in 'tun', 'worth', 'ham' and 'ley' are of Anglo-Saxon origins.

The Anarchy

Between 1135 and 1154 there was a succession crisis in England, characterised by a breakdown in law and order. Henry I named his daughter, the Empress Matilda, as his successor, but on Henry's death in 1135 his nephew Stephen de Blois took power with the help of his brother, Henry of Winchester. Stephen's early reign was marked by fierce fighting in the south-west of England. In 1139, the Empress Matilda invaded further north with the help of her half-brother, Robert of Gloucester.

In 1140, Robert of Gloucester and the army of the Empress Matilda succeeded in breaking through the town wall and went on to attack Nottingham Castle, held by King Stephen. Gloucester's army failed to take the castle, but they set fire to the town, subjecting the wretched townsfolk to all sorts of tortures in their search for

Saint Peter's church where the parishioners were slaughtered.

loot. They even massacred the parishioners of St Peter's who had taken refuge in the church trusting to the inviolability of the building to save them. With no respect for the sanctity of this holy place, Gloucester's army pursued their victims into the church and slaughtered them within the sacred precincts.

In 1141, Stephen was captured following the Battle of Lincoln, causing a collapse in his authority over most of the country, but neither side was able to achieve a decisive advantage and the war dragged on for many years. Henry reinvaded in 1153 and much of Nottingham was destroyed by fire. That same year, Stephen and Henry agreed a negotiated peace in which Stephen recognised Henry as his heir. Stephen died the following year and, on 8 December 1154, Henry presented himself as the legitimate heir to Henry I and was crowned Henry II of England alongside his wife, Queen Eleanor of Aquitaine.

The nineteen years of Stephen's reign had been a chaotic and troubled period, and Henry II commenced his reign by rebuilding his kingdom. England had suffered extensively during the war and Henry II began the long period of reconstruction.

3

NOTTINGHAM IN THE TWELFTH CENTURY

From the tenth to the fourteenth century, Nottingham was the scene of numerous sieges and wars that had almost destroyed the town wall built by the Saxon Edward the Elder in AD 921. Under instruction from Henry II it was largely rebuilt in 1156, although the line of this later town wall was of a much smaller circumference than the one erected previously by Edward the Elder. Edward's AD 924 bridge over the River Trent had also seen some fair wear and tear, and by 1156, was ready to be superseded by another bridge. The name of the bridge is variously spelt as 'Heck', 'Heth' or 'Heath-Beth' Bridge. It's conceivable that it was 'Health Bath Bridge', due to having adjacent bathing places – on the north for males and on the south for females. In 1274, there was a chapel, proseuche or oratory dedicated to St Mary (or St James) on Heth Beth Bridge, it's possible siting being on a plot of ground at the south end of the bridge called Lady Bay. It later became Lady Bay Toll Bar.

This was a time of much rebuilding in Nottingham. The wooden motte-and-baily castle was replaced by a far more defensible stone castle. It would have been imposing and of a complex architectural design, which eventually comprised an upper bailey at the highest point of the castle rock, a middle bailey to the north, which contained the main royal apartments, and a large outer bailey to the east. Castle yard was at an altitude of 110 feet, the castle parapet at 171 feet. Castle Rock would have been a honeycomb of natural caves, but man-made passages and dungeons would have been constructed in Norman times as necessary appurtenances of the castle.

Nottingham Castle subsequently became one of the greatest fortresses of medieval England. It was described at this time by historian William of Newburgh as being so strong by nature and art as to be able to defy any force but that of hunger. In the Middle Ages, it was a major royal fortress and occasional royal residence. For centuries the castle served as one of the most important in England for nobles and royalty alike. It was in a strategic position due to its location near a crossing of the River Trent, and it was also known as a place of leisure, being close to the royal hunting grounds of the Royal Forest of the Peak, the Royal Forests of Barnsdale and the Royal Forest of Sherwood. The castle also had its own deer park in the area immediately to the west, which is still known as The Park. Park Row was anciently called Butt Dykes because

The impressive entrance to Nottingham Castle.

the butt for the archery, which was compulsory on all Sundays and holidays, was set up in the dyke or ditch outside the town wall in the time of Henry II.

Nottingham Market Charter

In 1155, King Henry II gave Nottingham a charter. In the Middle Ages, a charter was a document granting the townspeople certain rights. Edward I gave the town a charter in 1284. In these charters, medieval Nottingham was given the right to hold a weekly market (twice weekly in 1284) and an annual fair in the Market Square. In those days, a fair was like a market but it was held only once a year for a period of a few days. Those early fairs were the predecessor of St Matthew's Fair, held annually on 27 September. In 1284, it was renamed the Nottingham Goose Fair to reflect the fact that it was predominantly an agricultural fair. The name is derived from the large number of geese (15,000 to 20,000) brought from neighbouring counties to be sold at the market. The journey for these geese from the Lincolnshire Fens and Norfolk took weeks, and the geese were shod with tar and sand to protect their feet. They were probably herded in through Goose Gate – an eastern entrance into the town and a name that still survives.

In the early days, the centrepoint of the square between the French borough and the English borough was divided by a wall. In the year 2,000, almost 1,000 years after that division, the old positioning of this historic wall was reinstated when a stainless steel drainage channel down the centre of the square was created to mark the position of the old wall.

Round the Market Square were streets that still retain their early names – Beast Market Hill to the west, Smithy Row to the north and South Parade to the south. Castle Gate was one of the four medieval streets that ran from the castle to the market place, which was originally the town green. Many streets were named after the medieval craftsmen. These included brewers, bakers, carpenters, shoemakers, tilers, potters, blacksmiths and goldsmiths.

Fletcher Gate is now a main thoroughfare running north from the Broadmarsh Centre, yet it still retains its name from the days when this street housed the workshops of the bowyers (bow makers) and fletchers (arrow makers). Tradesmen built their workshops at the front of the building where they and their family lived. The fletchers would be very selective about the wood they chose to make their arrows. It had to combine strength and lightness, and black poplar was especially good. Each shaft or stele would be between 27–35 inches long. One end held the flights made of goose feathers, or peacock feathers for the rich. These were stuck on with pitch and tied with silk or linen thread. The other end of the stele had an iron arrowhead made by the local blacksmith and attached with glue made from bluebell bulbs.

In 1285, Bridlesmith Gate was referred to as Lorimers Street from the Latin word *Lorimerius-Lorimer* – a maker of bits and bridles. It was in this area where the town mint was situated, but the actual site of this has been lost. During the nineteen-year war between Stephen and Henry, both sides had minted their own currency, causing financial chaos. Henry needed to remedy this. The Nottingham mint was in existence as late as the reign of King John, and for this privilege Nottingham paid the king an additional 40 s (£2) in coinage. There is frequent mention of payments of gold, or gold and silver mixed. The penny was in silver and so were the triens and farthings; the styca was of copper or brass.

King Richard and the Crusades

On the death of King Henry II, his son Richard became King of England for ten years from 1189–99, but during that time he only spent six months in England. He couldn't even be bothered to speak English, only French. He was known as Richard Coeur de Lion or Richard the Lionheart because of his reputation as a great military leader and warrior. By the age of sixteen, he had taken command of his own army.

When the Muslims tore down or spoiled many holy shrines and places considered holy by the Christians, the result was a series of holy wars. Although many didn't survive, to fight in the Holy Land and rescue Jerusalem from the Muslims meant treasures beyond belief in material and spiritual form. Those who went to fight wore the sign of the cross, and from the Latin word for cross comes *crux* and the name for the wars – the Crusades. There were eight crusades between 1095–1270, plus the children's crusade in 1212.

On 21 January 1188, after receiving news of the fall of Jerusalem to Saladin, Prince Richard decided to go to the third crusade. The fact that he became King the following year made no difference. He cared nothing about his royal duties and used his kingdom as a source of revenue to support his armies. Richard gave his brother John authority to rule England in his absence, but history has painted Prince John as a bad lot because, among other things, he plotted to take the crown for himself.

England was still run on the feudal system that had been introduced by William the Conqueror. This was based on the idea that every person in the land had a lord to whom he owed loyalty and certain services. The lords were usually answerable to powerful barons who had to provide fighting men from their lands and a steady income of money in the form of taxes for the Royal Coffers – always empty by expensive wars.

While Richard the Lionheart was away on the Third Crusade, a great number of English noblemen were away with him. Nottingham Castle was then occupied by the sheriff and, at this time, Ralph Murdach was High Sheriff of Nottinghamshire and Derbyshire. He was a rich cordwainer (an archaic name for a shoemaker or leather worker) who had bought his office from the grasping Bishop of Ely. The job of the high sheriff was to administer the law and collect the King's taxes, but Ralph Murdach embarked upon a relentless campaign of high taxation to repay his own debt. The sheriff had a contingent of troops and the use of Nottingham Castle, but would have lived at the Red Lodge at the end of what is now Angel Row.

Throughout his term of office, Ralph Murdach remained loyal to Prince John. In the 1190s, in one of his attempts to usurp the throne, Prince John made Nottingham Castle his headquarters. Ralph Murdach held Nottingham Castle in the name of Prince John until King Richard returned to England in 1194/95. Most of the men who held castles in the name of Prince John fled the country in fear of the King's vengeance, but those who held the castle at Nottingham steadfastly refused to relinquish it to the King's councillors. The King marched to Nottingham at the head of a vast army and besieged the castle with the siege machines he had used at Jerusalem. Richard was aided by Ranulph de Blondeville, 4th Earl of Chester, and David of Scotland, 8th Earl of Huntingdon.

The outer walls of the castle were quickly reduced to ruin. Many of the defenders and those who refused to surrender were captured and hanged in full sight of the castle. Two days later, those left inside laid down their arms and admitted defeat.

On Richard's deathbed, he named John his successor and he became king in 1199–1216. John's reign was not all bad for the country; many towns were given charters and encouraged to govern themselves. The towns benefited from changes in the way taxes were paid and could get income from taxing market traders entering the town.

Ye Olde Trip to Jerusalem

We can't possibly leave the subject of the Crusades without mentioning Ye Olde Trip to Jerusalem Inn at the foot of Castle Rock. Along with Ye Olde Salutation Inn and The Bell, it claims to be one of the oldest drinking establishments, not just in Nottingham but in England. It asserts to have been established in AD 1189, but there is no documentation to verify this date and the main building, built on the foundations of earlier constructions, was built in the sixteenth and seventeenth century.

According to local legend, it takes its name from the twelfth-century crusades to the Holy Land. The word 'trip' does not necessarily mean an entire journey – it's derived from an older meaning of the word, a stop during a journey. Knights who answered the call of Richard I to join the crusades stopped off at this watering hole for a tankard of ale and a break in the journey to the Holy Land. It was even claimed that

Ye Olde Trip to Jerusalem claims to date back to the crusades.

Richard himself frequented the pub, although that was probably a bit of propaganda by the landlord at the time.

The pub is famous for its caves carved out of the soft sandstone rock against which the building is set. The larger ground-level caverns are now used as the pub's rear drinking rooms. There is also a network of caves beneath the building, originally used as a brewhouse for the castle. They seem to date from the early eleventh century, around the time of the construction of the Norman castle. The brewhouse of the castle was separated from Ye Olde Trip to Jerusalem by King James I through an individual grant.

4

ROBIN HOOD –
NOTTINGHAM'S HERO

At this time, a vast area of Nottinghamshire was woodland with only wild and uncertain tracks and occasional clearings known as dales, which made it possible for a few diminutive villages to spring up. The inhabitants of these villages scratched a living from the dry, sandy Sherwood soil and lived on the primitive trades of the forest as charcoal burners, colliers and woodmen. Yet things were about to change radically. William the Conqueror, governing like a military dictator, established the term 'Royal Forest' when he claimed around ninety areas where all timber and game was the property of the King. From then on, successive kings and the Norman aristocracy enjoyed exclusive privilege of the chase.

Robin Hood striking a familiar pose.

To uphold these rules, a system of fines, taxes and licenses known as Forest Law were imposed and maintained by Norman henchmen with a severity previously unknown in England. The punishment for infringement of the forest laws was barbarous; a man could 'answer with his body' – a phrase that encompassed hanging and such mutilation as castration and blinding. Whole villages were starving, yet they were fined as a penalty for the unexplained disappearance of a deer. Against this background of unrest and inequality, in the forest theatre of Sherwood, the stage was set for the appearance of the celebrated Robin Hood and his companions to perform their own kind of forest rule.

The People's Hero

The peasants needed a hero they could identify with, a man of the time who waged a perpetual war against the powerful Norman barons, defied the unjust laws, ridiculed authority and robbed the rich to feed the poor. It didn't matter to the masses that nothing was written down. The balladeers and minstrels picked up the news wherever they went and passed it on in song. They were the reporters of the day who observed and recorded everyday events with uncanny accuracy. These news-carriers were entertainers who related the activities of Robin Hood and his men in rhyme and rhythm. They became the pop songs of the day, soon learnt, easily retained, enthusiastically recalled and sung by the people to ease the pain of daily labour. With the exploits of Robin Hood, the wandering minstrels had a winning formula. They wove a patchwork of fact and fiction into the contemporary culture of the time and were constantly seeking a new twist to an old story to add to their repertoire and please an ever-growing audience.

By 1340, the ballads had obviously circulated far because the Scottish historian Fordum wrote, in reference to Robin Hood and his men, 'The foolish and vulgar are delighted to hear the jesters and minstrels sing them above all other ballad.'

The legends and stories of Robin and his outlaw band were obviously far older than the first written mention – a collection of stories or fables with the Latin title *The Lytell Geste of Robyn Hode* (the deeds and history of Robin Hood). These stories, set to music, were told in rhyming verse in the vernacular spoken in the streets, yet each had a strong moralistic tone with a pious conclusion often added at the end.

In 1476, William Caxton set up the first printing press in England, printing school books and cheap editions of popular works. The term 'Chap book' is applied to these small, cheap booklets that usually consisted of twenty-four pages and were sold by 'peddlers' – cheap, chep or chap-men who also sold broadsheets and ballads. The stories of Robin Hood went into print, laying down the foundation of a saga that has endured the succeeding centuries and been perpetuated by each generation since. Books, plays, pantomimes, operas, TV, film and big screen productions have continued to embellish and develop the story until Robin Hood has become the most popular and best-known outlaw hero in the world. The legendary halo that has gathered round his name has resulted in a timeless fascination with Robin and his outlaw gang,

But who was Robin Hood – nobleman, yeoman or peasant? For hundreds of years, historians have picked at a hazy jumble of assorted evidence to try to pin down Robin's existence, status and origins to a specific person, time and place. In 1521, John Major placed Robin against the dates 1160–93 during the reign of Richard the Lionheart, and over the years this has been accepted by most people.

Elizabethan playwright Anthony Munday published two plays on the life of Robin Hood, proclaiming him the Earl of Huntington. The family had been Lords of Huntingdon. Their home, lands and earldom had been given by David son of the Scottish King around 1066 when their forefathers rose against the Normans.

William Stukeley attempted to authenticate the Huntington title by tracing their ancestry. In 1746 he produced a family tree showing that the Earl of Huntington, during the reign of Richard I, had the name Robert Fitz Othe. Robert is often shortened to Robin and the name Fitz was given to the illegitimate son of a nobleman, showing that royal blood flowed through their veins. Drop the Fitz and we have Robin Othe. Local dialect could pronounce Othe as 'Uth', and from that it's very easy to modify the name to Robin Hood, particularly as the 'th' sound in Middle English was often written as a letter 'D'.

In 1795, the antiquarian Joseph Ritson was so convinced of Robin Hood's historicality that he attempted a biography culminating in the *Life of Robin Hood*. The concept that Robin was an unjustly disinherited earl driven from his estates and forced to live as an outlaw alongside the peasants added to the pastoral charm of the tales. There is every possibility that the name Robin Hood was a nickname to hide his true identity and protect his family. However, people still say that Robin and his men have been forged by imaginative ballad makers rather than by factual circumstances. Sadly, the sparse information we have has been mulled over, changed and distorted

Robin Hood, the people's hero.

over the centuries, so we will never know for sure. As one learned historian said, 'If Robin Hood hadn't existed we would have needed to invent him.'

Nottingham's Superstar

Robin Hood was the people's hero, but over the years there has been controversy as to where he was actually based. It is accepted that he lived in Sherwood Forest, which extended from Nottingham in the south to Doncaster in the north, so both Nottinghamshire and Yorkshire have a claim to the forest hero. Robin Hood is generally associated with Nottingham and Nottinghamshire, his main adversary being the Sheriff of Nottingham. There is no doubt that the sheriff and Robin Hood were arch-enemies, and Robin never seemed to pass an opportunity to enrage and humiliate the man. While it's questionable whether the legend is based on fact or fiction, the way it weaves into the history of Nottingham can't be ignored. Robin would pass in and out of Nottingham to pray at St Mary's church (*Robin Hood and the Monk*), enter competitions (*Robin Hood and the Silver Arrow)*, sell meat (*Robin Hood and the Butcher)* and sell pots *(Robin Hood and the Potter)*.

5

CHURCHES AND CHARITIES

The limits of the borough of Nottingham at this time comprehended the three parishes of St Mary, St Peter and St Nicholas, and small parts of the parishes of Wilford and Bridgeford. The early Britons were Christians and preserved their faith from generation to generation. In its earliest stage, Christianity survived complete with associated relics, churches and rites even under domination.

St Mary's Church

In the Domesday Book of 1086 there is just one church mentioned in Nottingham. This was probably St Mary's and the priest was named as Aitard. St Mary's church is believed to date back to early Saxon times, making it the oldest religious foundation and the largest medieval building in the city of Nottingham. It was around St Mary's

St Mary's church dates back to pre-Norman times.

church that the English borough was established in the Norman period in what we now know as High Pavement at the heart of the historic Lace Market. St Mary's church was mentioned by name in 1103–08 when it featured in the foundation charter of Lenton priory. It remained the property of Lenton priory from 1108 to 1538, and the monks took the living of the church as rector and appointed a vicar to perform the daily offices. In *Robin Hood and the Monk* Robin goes to pray at St Mary's church, but is recognised by a monk who he had robbed of £100. The monk alerted the sheriff and Robin was thrown into the dungeon under Nottingham castle.

In the Middle Ages, the churches ran the only hospitals. In 1232, St Mary's hospital was founded and there was a hospital dedicated to St Thomas. There were also two leper hostels outside the gates of Nottingham dedicated to St Leonard and St Mary where the monks cared for the sick and the poor as best they could.

The main body of the present St Mary's church, which is at least the third build on the site, dates from the end of the reign of Edward III (1377) to Henry VII (1485–1509). It is likely that the south aisle wall was the first part of the building to be constructed in the early 1380s. The nave was finished before 1475 and is notable for its uniformity of Gothic perpendicular style. The remainder of the nave, the transepts and the tower, date from the early fifteenth century. The font is also fifteenth century and bears the rather unusual inscription 'wash sins not face only'. The church was closed for five years from 1843 for a major restoration.

In 1513, a free school was founded in the church by Dame Agnes Mellers. This is now Nottingham High School. In 1751, St Mary's pioneered Sunday School education for those children unable to attend a day school. Pupils were taught reading, writing and arithmetic, as well as religious knowledge. This was thirty-five years before the generally acknowledged first Sunday School was founded in Gloucester.

The twenty-five-year-old George Fox, founder of the Religious Society of Friends commonly known as the Quakers, arrived in Nottingham in 1649 where he proceeded to interrupt the service in St Mary's church. Through this misdemeanour he was cast into prison, which he described as 'a nasty stinking place'. Mrs Reckless, wife of John Reckless, sometime Sherriff of Nottingham who resided at the Sheriff's house in Spaniel Row, was present at St Mary's on the occasion of this interruption. She was so influenced by Fox's testimony that she arranged for him to be removed from the gaol in the custody of her husband at the Sheriff's house. Both the Sheriff and his wife soon afterwards accepted the Quaker faith and Sheriff Reckless himself preached in Nottingham Market Place.

St Mary's opened a workhouse in 1726 at the south end of Mansfield Road and ran it until 1834 when responsibility for workhouses was transferred from parishes to secular Boards of Guardians. The workhouse was demolished in 1895 to clear part of the site needed for the construction of the Victoria railway station.

St Peter's Church

St Peter's church dates back to Norman days and, although the original church believed to date from 1100 was destroyed by fire, St Peter's is one of the three medieval parish churches in Nottingham. It was St Peter's and St Nicholas' that formed the two churches within the French borough of Norman Nottingham. As they are not mentioned in the Domesday Book, it is believed that St Peter's church was founded almost immediately after the Conquest to provide religious accommodation for William Peveril's French castle-guard and their dependants who had settled in the new French borough round the castle. The church shows traces of many stages of construction from around 1180 onwards, with a number of the stones in the south arcade of the church bearing Norman tool marks. These are undoubtedly part of this original church, which is now Grade I listed as a building of outstanding architectural and historic interest.

There is mention of St Peter's church in 1141 when parishioners tried to take sanctuary in the church during the period known as The Anarchy, 1135–54.

The tower contains eight bells that were recast in 1771. A rather interesting story is attached to the seventh bell, which was presented in 1543 by Margaret Doubleday, one of the town's washerwomen. Together with a legacy of 20s (£1) for the sexton, her wishes were for the bell to be rung at four o'clock every morning to rouse the town's washerwomen so that they would not be late for their work. There is another rather charming old custom that is unique to St Peter's – the preaching of certain sermons. The Armada sermon dating from 1588 is read on the nearest Sunday to 28 July, and the Gunpowder Plot sermon from 1605, preached on the nearest Sunday to 5 November.

The Church of St Nicholas

A church of St Nicholas was erected on the site of the present building soon after the Conquest, and in appearance it seems to have been very much like St Peter's church, built around the same time. Very little is recorded about this early church, but in the thirteenth century what we now know as St Nicholas Street was called Jew Lane because so many Jews lived in the ghetto in this part of the Norman borough. When the Jews were banished from the country in 1290, the street took the name of the nearby church. In the tales of Robin Hood, Robin is said to have used St Nicholas' church as a hideout.

In 1642, during the Civil War, a body of Cavaliers acting for the king established themselves in the tower of St Nicholas church. From there, they had a direct line to the castle and for five days and nights they proceeded to bombard the Roundhead garrison. Col Huchinson managed to hold Nottingham Castle for the Parliamentarians, but the bombardment had been so exhaustive that when it was finally over, rather than risk another similar attack, it was ordered that the old church should be completely destroyed.

The homeless congregation were accommodated in a loft over the nearby St Peter's chancel for thirty-five years while the site of St Nicholas remained vacant. At last the building of a new church began in 1671 and was finished in 1678, giving the nucleus of the building we see today. Since then it has undergone a number of alterations and improvements. In the eighteenth century, St Nicholas' church was known as the Drawing Room church – a name it derived from those well-to-do people who lived in the parish and attended services there.

The church of St Nicholas.

All Saints' Church

Although a newcomer in comparison to the previous three churches, All Saints' church is Victorian and Grade II listed. It became one of the two churches of the parish of Nottingham when St Peter and All Saints' merged in December 2002. Following a further merger in September 2007, it became one of three parish churches within the parish of All Saints', St Mary's and St Peter's, Nottingham. The church was built in 1863/64, mainly in sandstone and in Gothic Revival style. It was consecrated on 3 November 1864. The architect was Thomas Chambers Hine of Nottingham.

Lenton Priory

The Cluniac house of Lenton priory, just west of The Park in the suburbs of Nottingham, was founded by William Peveril 'in honour of the Holy Trinity, and for the good of the souls of his lord King William and all his ancestors'. He gave the house to the church of Cluny in France. Usually a priory would pay a proportion of its income to its mother-house, which in this case was Cluny abbey in France, but William Peveril established in the foundation charter that Lenton priory would be free from the obligation to pay tribute to Cluny, 'save the annual payment of a mark of silver as an acknowledgement'.

In this foundation charter, William Peveril substantially endowed the house with the township of Lenton and its appurtenances, including seven mills, the townships of Radford, Morton and Keighton with all their appurtenances, and whatever he had in Newthorpe and Papplewick, both in wood and plain, with the consent of King

Lenton priory.

Henry, he gave the Nottingham churches of St Mary, St Peter and St Nicholas, and the churches of Radford, Linby, and Langar. He gave the tithes of his fisheries in Nottinghamshire plus substantial tithes from property, land, colts and fillies, lead and venison in the Peak District in Derbyshire, Northamptonshire, Buckingham and Leicestershire.

Its endowments, greater than those of any other monastic foundation in the county, added to its influence, so while Nottingham castle remained a construction of wood and earth, less than a mile away the priory of Lenton was built in the massive stonework of the Norman style. When the vast estates of the Peveril's, including Nottingham Castle, were confiscated to the crown in the reign of Henry II, Lenton priory was bestowed by the king on his second son, Prince John. In all probability, Lenton priory would have possessed a finer set of guest chambers than any that could be found in the town of Nottingham. Henry III lodged at the priory in 1230. Edward I sojourned there in April 1302 and again in April of the following year. Edward II visited the house for some days in the year of his accession, and again in 1323. Edward III was a royal visitor in 1336, as well as on other occasions.

However, it was because of its immense wealth that violent disagreements followed its seizure by the crown in the reign of Henry II. The priory was home mostly to French monks until the late fourteenth century when the priory was freed from the control of its foreign mother-house, but by then the priory was struggling financially and was noted for its poverty and indebtedness. The priory was dissolved as part of Henry VIII's Dissolution of the Monasteries. The Valor Ecclesiasticus of 1534 records the priory as having a gross income of £387 (10s 10½d) and considerable outgoings.

Lenton's last prior was Nicholas Heath who was appointed in 1535, but in February 1538 he was thrown into prison along with many of his monks. They were accused of high treason, most likely under the Verbal Treasons Act of December 1534. In March, Nicholas Heath with eight of his monks – Ralph Swenson, Richard Bower,

Richard Atkinson, Christopher Browne, John Trewruan, John Adelenton, William Berry and William Gylham – and four labourers of Lenton (probably servants of the priory) were indicted for treason. They were sentenced to be executed, hanged, drawn and quartered. There is reference to these executions in the chamberlain's accounts of Nottingham for 1537/38 – a charge of 2d was paid for clearing Cow Lane 'when the monks of Lenton suffered death'. That would indicate that the sentences were carried out in the marketplace as Cow Lane was one of the principal approaches; the name was altered to Church Street in 1812. On an equally repugnant note, some of the quarters of those executed were displayed outside the priory.

Because Lenton Priory was dissolved by attainder, not a single monk or servant of the house obtained a pension. Even the five paupers maintained there in accordance with the charter of the time of Henry I were thrust out penniless.

After the Dissolution, many former monasteries were turned into farms or houses of the gentry, but the site so near to Nottingham was a handy source of stone and architectural material to be used in other nearby buildings. The site was eventually bought by William Stretton in 1802, who built a house there. When William died, the property passed to his sons Sempronius and Severus, who sold the house to the Sisters of Nazareth in 1880. With the rapid growth of industrialisation in the eighteenth and nineteenth century, the population of Lenton rose from 893 in 1801 to 23,872 in 1901. The Sisters of Nazareth sold the property in the early years of the twenty-first century, and the site was redeveloped for housing to meet this exceptional need. All that now remains are elements of the chapel of the monastic hospital incorporated into the priory church of St Anthony, Lenton, fragments of a stone column where Old Church Street meets Priory Street, the twelfth-century font in Holy Trinity church, Lenton, floor tiles in Nottingham Castle Museum and stained glass in Nuthall church.

The Carmelite Friars
The Carmelite Friars are first heard of in the twelfth century, and tradition has it that when the Crusaders got through to Mount Carmel they found a religious organization living there who said they were descendants of Elisha. They wore a white cloak in memory of Elijah's mantle and became known as the White Friars. Their full name was the Order of the Brothers of Our Lady of Mount Carmel, or Carmelites. The order was introduced into England sometime around 1245 and they were established in Nottingham in 1276 by Reginald Lord Gray of Wilton. They were given property, which gradually increased until it covered a substantial area around Friary Lane in the centre of Nottingham. It had its boundary wall along Beastmarket Hill and the foundations of this wall were discovered in 1923, as were many remains of the daily life of the Carmelite Friars.

Part of their property included a guesthouse/refectory on the site of what is now The Bell Inn, Beastmarket Hill, on the west side of the Market Square. According to dendrochronologic dating of its timbers, the current building dates from around 1420. Like many Nottingham properties, there are natural and hand-hewn caves under the property used as cellars. These date back to at least the twelfth century when they were excavated by the Carmelite Friars, but there is a small cave reputed to be Anglo-Saxon.

The cellars contain two wells, one aptly named Monks Well, from where the brethren drew the water to brew the monastic ales.

In 1316, King Edward II gave the Carmelite Friars the chapel of St James, located on St James Street, central Nottingham. The chapel had originally been built by William Peveril for the use of the garrison of the castle, and granted to Lenton priory. The Friary, like all other monastic institutions, was dissolved by Henry VIII and the property and lands were granted to Humphrey Strelley who sold it to John Manners, the younger son of the Earl of Rutland, around 1573.

John Manners married Dorothy Vernon, the daughter of Sir George Vernon of Haddon Hall, Derbyshire, ancestors of the current Dukes of Rutland. Dorothy eloped with John and, in the popular imagination, they moved into the old priory, which became known as Dorothy Vernon's House. It's highly unlikely as the Manners owned many properties in Nottingham. Thomas Manners, Earl of Rutland, was the Constable of Nottingham Castle in 1622. The family name was given to Rutland Street, Rutland Gardens and Granby Street. The Marquis of Granby is the title of the eldest son and frequently the name given to popular pubs belonging to the family. The 400-year-old hostelry known as the Talbot on Long Row has an unbroken history of serving refreshment. Talbot is another family name. The Tudor Inn was demolished in 1874 by Edward Cox who created the most ornate gin palace in the Midlands with extravagant decorations and statuary. It's now a Yates wine bar.

Dorothy Vernon's house, part of the former Carmelite Friary.

Road widening in Friar Lane, which began in 1922, made it necessary to demolish the buildings on the eastern side of Friar Yard. Dorothy Vernon's House was lost, and with it any evidence of the ancient chapel of St James and the Carmelite or White Friars' House of Nottingham.

The Bell Inn

In 1539, following the Dissolution of the Monasteries, the part that had been the Carmelite guesthouse/refectory became a secular alehouse taking its name from the Angelus Bell that hung outside. *Angelus* is Latin for Angel (a former name of the inn), and the ringing of the Angelus Bell was closely associated with reciting the triple Hail Mary – the origin of our modern Angelus.

The earliest known written reference to the Inn is the 1638 will of Alderman Robert Sherwin, which bequeathed the leasehold of the establishment to the poor of the local parishes. John White bequeathed the freehold of the Inn to his wife Mary in 1732 and two years later she sold it to the Smiths – the wealthy local banking family.

In 1779, the Bell was one of the inns selected as a suitable billet for men of the Royal Regiment of Horse Guards (The Blues). The last recorded guests were four dragoons that spent the night there in 1748 for 3s. Jane Lart purchased the freehold from the Smiths in 1803 and the leasehold from the church in 1806. Under the terms of the lease, she also undertook extensive repairs of the building and constructed a Georgian frontage that allowed for the preservation of the rare crown post structure, which is still there today.

In 1812, the cricketer William Clarke gave up his bricklaying job to become landlord of the Bell Inn, then moved on to the Trent Bridge Inn where he established the famous cricket ground (*see Trent Bridge Inn*). On Goose Fair night in 1831, rioters protesting against the Reform Act gathered at the Inn. They were in a destructive mood and, having smashed the windows, went on the rampage, burning down many of the city's prominent buildings, including Nottingham Castle and Colwick Hall. Ten years later, in 1841, Tory politician John Walters established his campaign headquarters at the inn for the general election and had to take refuge here when he was set upon by an angry mob in the Square.

In 1888, the inn was sold to A. W. Hickling and was subsequently sold to Joseph Jackson in 1898 – a family ownership that has lasted over 100 years. In 1982, the inn became a Grade II listed building and has retained many interesting features. Entrance to the bars is via the central passageway that has retained its original flagstones along which travellers used to lead their horses to the stables. There was an outer courtyard with two wells, the water from which was used for brewing. To the right of the entranceway are the leprosy windows where customers supposedly had their fingers counted before being allowed to enter. The oak-panelled, low-beamed rooms feature an original fireplace and a large stained-glass window. The original timber crown posts and cross beams dating back to 1437 have been preserved and there are many historical artefacts on display.

The Inn was featured along with its rivals Ye Olde Trip to Jerusalem Inn and Ye Olde Salutation Inn in an episode of the channel 4 TV series *History Hunters*.

The research team used records, building architecture and local legends to decide which was truly the oldest. No decision was made.

Plumptre Hospital/Almshouses

Plumptre Hospital in Plumptre Square was founded in 1392 while Richard II was on the throne. It's benefactor was John de Plumptre, sometime Mayor of Nottingham who came to Nottingham in the thirteenth century. The family lived in an imposing house on the site recently occupied by the Flying Horse Hotel, The Poultry, described as an Elizabethan coaching inn. It bears the date 1483. Its gardens would have extended to St Peter's Gate and probably Peck Lane was a side way into their premises. Much restored, the façade was redesigned in 1934 with plasterwork to give the building a Tudor appearance. In 1967 an application to demolish the inn was refused but in 1987 permission was granted for it to be converted into a shopping arcade.

Plumptre hospital/almshouses supported two priests, and were dedicated to the Blessed Virgin Mary. John Plumptre decreed that it was for the sustenance of – 'thirteen poor women broken down of age and depressed of poverty', although, in 1414, the number was reduced to seven. It was one of the few charities to escape the great pillage under Edward VI. In 1547, when the endowments of nearly all charitable institutions were swept away. It was managed so well that the commissioners appointed for the purpose could find no fault to justify them in confiscating its funds.

The building was renovated in 1560, two years after Queen Elizabeth commenced her reign, by Huntingdon Plumptre. He raised the rents and gave the widows a respectable allowance of 5s per month, with sixpence extra at New Year. It was enlarged in 1753 by another John Plumptre so that it could take thirteen widows. In addition to the New Year sixpence, they each received £13 10s per year, a gown and a tonne of coal. Although the Plumptre family moved to Kent in 1756, they continued to support the charity by rebuilding the hospital again in 1823, but by 1991 the charity no longer had the resources. Plumptre Hospital had been providing almshouse accommodation for 599 years.

Collins Almshouse

This block of buildings was purpose built in 1709 by Thomas Smith Jnr, the banker who was acting as trustee under the will of Abel Collin. Originally, the charity was for twenty-four tenants and, in addition to a house, each beneficiary was provided with a small pension and a supply of coals. The trust was managed so well that not only were the number of houses in Park Street increased by a second block facing Houndsgate, but other almshouses were erected in Carrington Street. Many other charities were established, with the increased and ever-increasing income from the estate. The block was demolished in 1950 with the building of Maid Marion Way.

6

TRADE IN THE MIDDLE AGES

Nottingham was a major centre of trading and craftsmanship during the middle ages. Many merchants would have navigated along the Trent with their produce. The charter of 1155 allowed the burgesses to charge tolls to merchants entering the town and for those using parts of the Trent.

Tile-making and pottery had been established in Nottingham by the thirteenth century and possibly earlier. When the Victoria railway station was being excavated in April 1897, in the area of Parliament Street, the old town wall was cut through. It was near this point, at a depth of 3–4 m below the original surface, that an ancient pottery kiln and pottery was discovered. The pottery was in pieces but consisted of jugs, stew jars and drinking vessels made of coarse clay and reddish brown in colour. They had been made on a potter's wheel. There was no ornamentation except that the handles were indented or grooved the whole length by the potter's thumb, presenting a very crude attempt at foliation.

The wall found here was the one built in 1090 to divide the French and English boroughs, extending down what is now Mansfield Road to the River Trent. The Norman invaders occupied the western side of this wall; the Saxons and Danes occupied the eastern side of the wall. The pottery and kiln was found on the eastern side close to the wall, so connecting the two it is feasible that the period of the kiln and pottery could be Anglo-Norman, dating to the eleventh century.

Trade Names

Many trades, where one or more craftsmen would have been employed, are reflected in the town's street names. Some are more obvious than others. Tanning was an important trade in Nottingham, even into the post-medieval period. There would have been one or more tanneries on Tanners Street where animal skins were processed. Leather tanning is the process of converting raw hides or skins into leather. Hides and skins have the ability to absorb tannic acid (from which the tanning process draws its name) to prevent them from decaying, make them resistant to wetting and keep them supple and durable.

Barker Gate was also for the tanners and barkers. The tanners would soak and treat cattle skins before placing them in vats where they soaked in a mixture of alum, oak bark and urine. A barker was a tanner – a name derived from the old English 'barken' (the bark of a tree), which was used in the process. The tanning trade was based in Broad Marsh and Narrow Marsh where they were close to the River Leen for their water. They also worked in the caves beneath the streets in this area, and in the City Of Caves visitors can see the only medieval tannery still in existence.

Lister Gate (which was probably originally Litster) was where the litsters or dyers worked. This is from another old English word 'litster', meaning to dye. Dyeing cloth was a major trade in Nottingham. Dyes would have been supplied by spicers or apothecaries. The red for leather was obtained from brazil nuts, archil is a lichen that produced violet or purple dye, woad produced a blue dye, madder produced a red dye, verdigris produced a green dye and so on. The process, like tanning, was very smelly.

Pilcher Gate was for the sellers of furs or pilches – an outer garment made originally of skin or fur and later of leather or wool. Pilch is an obsolete name for a saddle cover and an infant's outer wrapping, worn over the napkin prior to the days of plastic pants.

Wheeler Gate was where the wheelwrights worked and Bridlesmith Gate, along with Great Smith Gate and Smithy Row, was where metalworking took place. Foundries existed in the town, and many everyday implements such as cauldrons, horseshoes, candlesticks and knives would have been made from iron, copper, steel, bronze, lead, latten and pewter. There were also gold and silversmiths, bell-founders and armourers.

Sheep Rearing and the Staple

Sheep rearing flourished around Nottingham thanks to the rich grazing grounds to be found in and around Sherwood Forest. Wool was a major industry in the area dating back to prehistoric times when the spinning of wool was a cottage industry. The sheep's fleece was washed and carded, then spun into thread on spinning wheels worked by unmarried females or spinsters, giving us a word that is still in use.

In medieval Nottingham the main industry was fulling the wool. Fulling is a step in woollen cloth making, which involves the cleansing of cloth – in this case wool – to eliminate oils, dirt and other impurities and make it thicker by matting the fibres. The thickened wool is felted – given strength and waterproofing. Originally, fulling was carried out by pounding the woollen cloth with the fuller's feet while ankle deep in human urine. Urine was so important to the fulling business that it was taxed. Stale urine, known as wash, was a source of ammonium salts and assisted in cleansing and whitening the cloth. By the medieval period, fuller's earth had been introduced for use in the process. Fuller's earth is a soft clay-like material occurring naturally as an impure hydrous aluminium silicate. It was used in conjunction with wash. Because they used their feet, the workers were called walkers (still used today as a surname) and the street where they worked was often named Walker Street. After this stage, water was used to rinse out the foul-smelling liquor used during cleansing. These processes were followed by stretching the cloth on great frames known as tenters, to which it was attached by tenterhooks. It's from this process that the phrase 'being on tenterhooks' is derived, meaning to be held in suspense.

From the medieval period, the fulling of cloth was often undertaken in water-driven fulling mills. The fact that there is a Walker Street off Windmill Lane at Sneinton might indicate that windmills were also used as a source of power for fulling.

Men have used waterpower since Roman times. The Domesday survey of 1086 shows there was a mill valued at 10s at Lenton. The name is derived from the River Leen, which runs nearby. The River Leen provided the waterpower for a score of mills in later centuries. Around the fifteenth century, the application of waterpower for fulling cloth was probably the greatest technical achievement, and along the river banks, industry would have relied upon the power of the river water.

The Merchant Staplers

From 1314, the crown required all wool for export to be traded at a designated market called 'The Staple'. This allowed the crown to monitor the trade and levy tax on exports. The Company of Merchants of the Staple of England, also known as the Merchant Staplers, was incorporated by Royal Charter in 1319, although the company of the staple may be able to trace its ancestry back as far as 1282 or even further. It is the oldest mercantile corporation in England dealing in wool, skins, lead and tin.

The Staple controlled the export of wool to the continent during the late medieval period, but after Calais was conquered in 1347 that became the staple. In exchange for the company's cooperation in the payment of taxes, the Staple of Calais was granted a total monopoly on wool exports from England. This was important to the English Crown, both as a source of revenue and through its role in the defence of Calais against the French. As domestic cloth production increased, raw wool exports were less important, diminishing the power of the merchants.

Thurland, Merchant of the Staple

One of the most prominent figures in the commercial, social and public life of Nottingham about the middle of the fifteenth century was Thomas Thurland. He was Merchant of the Staple, several times mayor, an alderman and a 'Keeper of the Peace'. Around 1458 he built Thurland Hall, a building so magnificent it was said to be second only in splendour to the castle. Thurland Hall was located on the north side of Gridlesmith Gate, now Pelham Street, and covered almost 9 acres, including what is now Thurland Street, named after him. Thurland was one of a number of men who benefitted greatly when Edward III (1336–60) incorporated the Merchants of the Staple, which was one of the most ancient companies of merchants in England. Thurland was a Merchant of the Staple, and became a very wealthy and important man in Nottingham. He was returned four times as Burgess in Parliament for Nottingham in 1441, 1448, 1449, and 1450. He was Mayor of Nottingham nine times between 1442–46. In 1457/58 he gave twenty loads of Basford stone for the repair of the 'Bridges of Hethbeth' (the early Trent Bridge) and was appointed a collector of alms for the bridge. During 1467–69, he was a 'Keeper of the Peace', or magistrate, and in 1472/73 the King appointed him as a commissioner for examining land and tenaments for the purpose of levying taxes on them. He died around 1474–77. Thurland Hall passed through a succession of wealthy and influential owners, including the newly-created Earl of Clare who changed the name to Clare Hall (*see Chapter 8*).

Nottingham Alabaster

A Nottingham industry that flourished from the fourteenth century until the early sixteenth century is the carving of alabaster sculpture. Alabaster carvers were at work in London, York and Burton-on-Trent, but the largest concentration was in Nottingham. This has led to all the English medieval output being referred to as Nottingham alabaster.

Alabaster is a mineral composed of gysum and various impurities. It is much softer and easier to work than marble. Carvings were made as single figures, assemblies for tomb monuments, including full-length effigies, but it's not suitable for outdoors use. The tomb in Westminster Abbey of John of Eltham, Earl of Cornwall, who died in 1334, is an early example of very high quality Nottingham Alabaster. Edward III commissioned an altarpiece or reredos for St George's chapel in Windsor in 1367, and in 1414 the architect mason of Rouen Cathedral was in Nottingham arranging for alabaster to be produced for his new church in northern France.

The most common survivals are panels from sets for altarpieces, which could be transported relatively easily and fitted into a locally made architectural surround of stone or wood on arrival at their destination. These were much in demand for the private chapels of the nobility. Nottingham alabaster images were hugely popular in Europe and were exported in large quantities, some ending up as far afield as Iceland, Croatia and Poland.

Most alabaster altarpieces and religious carvings in English churches were destroyed in the Reformation, and by the fifteenth century Nottingham had established itself as a centre of a thriving export trade in religious sculpture made from Nottingham Alabaster. The greatest export market was in France where even today some churches retain in situ their English alabaster altarpieces unlike England, where survivals are extremely rare. The sculptures were normally brightly painted, sometimes all over, sometimes partially, but much of the paint has often been lost and many pieces have had the rest completely removed by dealers, collectors or museums in the past.

The alabaster used in the industry was quarried largely in the area around South Derbyshire near Tutbury and Chellaston. The craftsmen were known by various names such as alabastermen, kervers, marblers and image makers. Around 1370, there was an alabasterman named Peter the Mason documented in Nottingham. Can we assume that he is the same Peter who, on 6 June 1371, received payment for an altarpiece? 'To Peter Maceon of Nottingham, the balance of 300 marks for a table (altar piece) of alabaster made by him and placed upon the High Altar within the free Chapel of Saint George of Windsor.' The execution of this order cost £200 and required ten carts, eighty horses and twenty men to transport it to its destination. The journey occupied seventeen days in the autumn of 1367 and the expenses of transport amounted to £30.

Alabaster images in English churches may have survived the Dissolution of the Monasteries in the 1530s, but most did not survive the reign of Edward I following the Putting Away of Books and Images Act 1549 ordering the destruction of all images.

Eight months after this act, in January 1550, the English Ambassador to France reported the arrival of three English ships laden with alabaster images to be sold at Paris, Rouen and elsewhere. Whether these were new images, or ones removed from English churches, is not clear. From the middle of the sixteenth century, the alabaster workshops focused instead on sculpting alabaster tombs and church monuments. The industry survived until the falling price of marble and exhaustion of most English quarries made alabaster increasingly rare as a material for English sculptors by the late eighteenth century.

The Victoria and Albert Museum and Nottingham Castle Museum hold the two principal collections of Nottingham alabaster in the United Kingdom. The collection in Nottingham Castle Museum includes three Nottingham alabaster figures, representing the Virgin Mary, St Peter and an unknown bishop. They were discovered during the demolition of St Peter's church, Flawford, Nottinghamshire, in 1779. It is thought that they would have been hidden under the floor around 1539 during the Dissolution of the Monasteries.

7

NOTTINGHAM CASTLE

The *Coup d'État* at Nottingham Castle

During the fourteenth century, Nottingham Castle was again used as a royal residence. Shortly before his eighteenth birthday, King Edward III, with the help of a few trusted companions led by Sir William Montagu, staged a *coup d'état* against his mother Isabella of France, and her lover, Roger Mortimer, 1st Earl of March. Both were acting as regents during Edward's minority following the murder of his father Edward II at Berkeley Castle. Sir William Montagu and his companions were accompanied by William Eland, castellan and overseer of Nottingham Castle, who knew the location of a secret tunnel that would take them up to a normally locked door higher up in the castle. In the dark of night on 19 October 1330, Montagu and his companions entered the tunnel and climbed up to the door, which had now been unlocked either by Edward or a trusted servant. They overpowered Mortimer and killed Mortimer's personal guards. Mortimer was bound and gagged, led out of the tunnel and arrested along with Queen Isabella. Mortimer was sent to the Tower of London and hanged a month later. Isabella was forced into retirement at Castle Rising Castle, and with this dramatic event the reign of Edward III began. The tunnel has since been given the name Mortimer's Hole.

A Victorian artist's impression of the guards entering the tunnels under the castle.

Mortimer's Hole

Mortimer's Hole is a tunnel 107 yards long, 7 feet high, 6 feet wide and a very steep descent. The entrance is in the café courtyard under a turret on the southern side of the castle. As it descends, the 300-odd sandstone steps carved as a spiral staircase can be both steep and quite slippery due to the loose sand.

The tunnel runs under the outer bailey walls and in places it exits onto the cliff walls. There are various openings in the rock southwards, not unlike portholes for guns, which is what they were used for during the Civil War. Canons were placed in the openings and behind in the deceptively roomy tunnel were the cannonballs and ammunition. For this reason, it has become known as the Gun Emplacement. As the tunnel exits at the bottom of the cliffs in the Brewhouse Yard near Ye Olde Trip to Jerusalem pub, it was probably used to deliver goods more easily into the castle, or for troops to smuggle women in for a bit of forbidden pleasure.

King David Held Prisoner at the Castle

In 1346, King David II of Scotland attacked England in support of France while Edward III was away fighting in France. The Scots were defeated at Neville's Cross near Durham where David was injured and taken prisoner in October 1346. He was held captive in Nottingham Castle dungeons for eleven years, during which time he reputedly drew what is now referred to as the Passion of Christ on his cell wall.

The openings in Castle Rock known as the Gun Emplacement.

In 1357, under the Treaty of Berwick, he was allowed to return to Scotland for a ransom of 100,000 marks. From this we obtained the phrase 'a king's ransom', although it seems that the full amount was never paid.

In 1365, Edward III improved the castle with a new tower on the west side of the middle bailey and a new prison under the High Tower. In 1376, Peter de la Mare, speaker of the House of Commons, was confined in Nottingham Castle for having 'taken unwarrantable liberties with the name of Alice Perrers, mistress of the king'. In 1387, the state council was held in the castle. Richard II held councils with the Lord Mayor of London, aldermen and sheriffs in the castle in 1392. The last visit recorded by Richard II was in 1397 when another council was held here.

The Salutation Inn, Hounds Gate

The Salutation Inn, at the corner of Hounds Gate and St Nicholas Street or Jew Lane as it was anciently called, dates *c.* 1240, with fourteenth century and later additions and rebuilds. Its outer walls are the original wattle and daub plaster, and inside are original oak beams in excellent state of preservation. The inn is built on earlier foundations. Underneath the building is a cave with a 70-foot well sunk into the rock. This cave system would have been in existence long before a building was even thought of. The name 'Salutation' is from the annunciation of the birth of Christ by the Archangel

The Salutation Inn dates back to *c.* 1240.

Gabriel to the Virgin Mary: '*Ave Maria, plene gratia*'. This sign was not infrequently associated with inns belonging to religious houses, so this inn may have been the guesthouse of either the Carmelite or the Franciscan friary of Nottingham.

The inn has many historical associations. It was used by members of the court of Edward III who used Nottingham Castle as a residence and held parliaments there. In 1336, when Edward III stayed at Nottingham Castle, many of his retinue were housed and fed at Ye House By Ye Sign Of Salutation. In 1642, when King Charles I raised his standard at Nottingham at the beginning of the Civil War, the inn was used as a recruiting office. During the coaching era, the inn had a sinister reputation as a hangout for highwaymen.

Nottingham Castle During the Fifteenth and Sixteenth Centuries

From 1403 until 1437, Nottingham Castle was the main residence of Henry IV's queen, Joan. In the latter half of the fifteenth century, it continued to grow in size and magnificence during the reigns of Edward IV (1461–83) and Richard III, the last Yorkist King. This was the time of the Wars of the Roses – a series of battles fought between the House of Lancaster and the House of York from 1455–85. The name is based on the badges used by the two sides – the red rose for the Lancastrians, the white rose for the Yorkists. Only with the Wars of the Roses did Nottingham Castle begin to be used again as a military stronghold. Edward IV proclaimed himself King in Nottingham, and in 1476 he ordered the construction of a new tower and royal apartments. It was from Nottingham castle that Richard III marched to meet Henry Tudor at Bosworth Field in 1485. Richard was defeated and Henry Tudor, founder of the house of Tudor, became King of England.

During the reign of King Henry VII, the castle remained a royal fortress. Henry VIII ordered new tapestries for the castle before he visited Nottingham in August 1511. By 1536, Henry had the castle reinforced and its garrison increased from a few dozen men to a few hundred. In 1540, Nottingham Castle was described by John Leland as 'the most beautifulest part and gallant building for lodging ... a right sumptuous piece of stone work.'

The castle at this time covered the Standard Hill area north-west of the castle now occupied by the general hospital. It joined the town wall at what is now the upper end of Park Row. Over on the west is Nottingham Park, which began life as the park of Nottingham Castle. Probably a small portion of the great Sherwood Forest was fenced in and kept stocked with game so that the sovereigns who happened to be in residence at Nottingham Castle could always have a recreational hunt close at hand. The Park sank from its high estate, and in 1508 is referred to as 'the cuny garth', or rabbit warren. South of the park was a large reservoir used as a fish pond/stew pond for the castle. It was probably established in the early Middle Ages when fresh fish would be a welcome change of diet during the long winter months. Around 1720, it was let to the Water Work Co., who used it as a reservoir until 1789 when it became silted up. Eventually, in 1791, it ceased to exist as a pond when it was used as a dump into which to throw the soil dug out for the foundation of the barracks in Barrack Lane. The site was found to be extremely fertile and was let out as allotments. The rock shelter on the site was used as a garden or fishing tackle store. The site has now been built over and Hope Drive and Fishpond Drive constructed on it.

Spaniel Row, like the nearby Hounds Gate just north of the castle, refers to the royal dogs kept here by various monarchs. The hounds were used for hunting, but the spaniels were a favourite dog of King Charles, a specific strain of which were given the name King Charles Spaniel.

The castle had ceased to be a royal residence by 1600. James I took the English throne in 1603 uniting Scotland and England, but during his reign Nottingham Castle deteriorated. In 1622, it was granted to the constable, Thomas Manners, Earl of Rutland who reported on the need for maintenance. A survey in 1625 stated: 'there is much dekay and ruyne of said castell ... part of the roof of the Great Hall is fallen down. Also the new building there is in dekay of timber, lead and glass'.

This was the beginning of the end of what was truly Nottingham Castle.

Nottingham in the Civil War

The Civil War was a conflict between King Charles I and Parliament. The Parliamentarians were known as Roundheads; the Royalists were Cavaliers. Bishop Trollope, in his paper on the 'Raising of the Standard', printed in the second series of *Old Nottinghamshire*, gives a detailed report of the happenings in Nottingham when he wrote:

> On the 16th of August, Charles the First reached Lincoln, on the 17th Newark, on the 18th Southwell, and on that night he arrived at Nottingham ... The King's arrival caused the greatest excitement, as most of the inhabitants were still, to a certain extent, Royalists ... Followed by a considerable body of cavalry, he was greeted by the loud shouts of the people as he passed on towards Thurland House, the Earl of Clare's residence in Nottingham, which had been prepared for his reception ... The next morning the King reviewed his cavalry – eight hundred strong, by ordering them to advance towards Coventry. The citizens of Coventry closed the gates of their town against the King's troops and the King himself ... Charles was forced to return baffled and disappointed. That night he slept at the house of Sir Thomas Leigh, of Stoneleigh. Such were the discouraging circumstances under which the King returned to Nottingham. Towards evening a procession was formed for the purpose of erecting the Standard on the highest tower of the Castle ... That night a violent storm arose, which blew down the Standard, which was regarded as an evil omen. Thinking that its retention within the Castle walls might have had something to do with their coldness of conduct, Charles determined to remove the Standard thence, and to repeat the ceremony of its erection. Hence three days later on the 25th August, Charles, attended by his train as before again rode from Thurland Hall to the Castle for the purpose of raising the Royal Standard again ... About a week after this event the King's stay at Nottingham reached its close ... The King left this town September 13th, 1642.

When the standard attracted few recruits it was moved outside the castle walls and set up on a rocky knoll, which in those days was called Hill Close, just north of the castle. The name has been changed to Standard Hill in memory of the occasion, and a commemorative stone at the corner of King Charles Street and Standard Hill just by the west door of St James's church now marks the spot.

By November, Parliamentary troops occupied Nottingham under the leadership of John Hutchinson. Col Hutchinson was born on High Pavement, Nottingham, and was educated at the Free School in Stoney Street. He married Lucy, daughter of Sir Allen Aspley, in 1638, and in 1643 he became governor of Nottingham Town and Castle. As a Parliamentarian, he took control of the site, made the castle more defensible and held it for the rest of the war despite attacks by the Royalist Army in June 1643 and January 1644. Throughout that time, his wife stayed with him. Her memoirs of that period are in the Castle Museum. She wrote:

> For five days and nights there is firing without intermission. Within the walls of the castle are not more than eighty men. The musketeers on St Nicholas' steeple pick off the cannoniers at their guns. Now and then as the assailants are beaten from the walls, they leave a wounded man behind and he is dragged into the castle. On the sixth day relief arrives. The Cavaliers are driven from the town with great slaughter and Nottingham Castle is filled with prisoners.

Lucy was not idle during those six days. Within the castle was a dungeon called the Lion's Den into which the prisoners were cast. As the men were carried bleeding to the dungeon, she implored that they should be brought to her and she bound up and dressed their wounds. 'I have done nothing but my duty', she told two fanatical ministers of the garrison who criticized her.

The Royalists were never able to retake the castle, but the number of skirmishes on the site meant that it was soon in a semi-ruined state. After the Battle of Worcester on 3 September 1651, when the future Charles II was overthrown and forced to flee abroad, the Royalists admitted defeat. After the execution of Charles I in 1649, the country was run by Oliver Cromwell who, in 1651, ordered that Nottingham Castle should be destroyed to prevent it ever falling into Royalist hands. His orders were carried out by Col John Hutchinson on behalf of Parliament. With the Restoration of the Monarchy in 1661, Col Hutchinson was imprisoned for having been one of the signatories of Charles I's death warrant. He died in captivity in 1664.

A New Build on the Castle Site

In 1663, the ruinous castle site was purchased by William Cavendish, the 1st Duke of Newcastle. The new build started in 1674 on the previous structure and was completed five years later by his son Henry Cavendish, the 2nd Duke, but sadly it is not very castle-like. He obviously decided to replace the medieval stronghold with a ducal palace in the continental baroque style, influenced no doubt by the fashionable residences that were being built in the area. The mason for the mansion was Samuel Marsh of Lincoln, who also worked for the Duke at Bolsover Castle. His designs are generally thought to have been strongly influenced by Ruben's engravings in his book

Palazzi di Genova. The Duke's mansion is a rare surviving example in England of mannerist architecture.

The gatehouse of the medieval castle and much of the walling of the outer bailey was retained as a garden wall for the Ducal mansion. However, the northernmost part of the outer bailey was lost when an approach road was constructed in the 1830s for the development of The Park Estate on the former deer park. The first house in the park was built on Newcastle Terrace in 1827, but it was around 1887 before the estate was completed. Architects from all over the world came to see it and many modern housing estates have been planned on similar lines. There are some 7 miles of private roads and access at one point is via a gated tunnel that passes under College Street, the Ropewalk, Newcastle Terrace and Newcastle Drive, for residents only.

This part of the castle site was later used for the expansion of Nottingham General Hospital. The founder of the hospital was John Key who left a legacy of £500 when he died in 1778. Of the 2-acre site at Derry Mount, one acre was given by the Duke, the other by the Nottingham Council and the hospital was opened in September 1782.

The new-build castle is not very castle-like.

8

NOTTINGHAM IN THE SEVENTEENTH CENTURY

This was a time when the local gentry, who had previously lived in the countryside, decided to move to town and build themselves substantial houses in the latest architectural styles. New houses were built in Castle Gate and Low Pavement. Thurland Hall, the former home of Thomas Thurland, was rebuilt and enlarged by Sir John Holles, 1st Earl of Clare, as his Nottingham residence. It became known as Clare Hall. James I is reputed to have stayed there in 1612 and Charles I in 1634 and 1642, when it was described as the largest and most ancient mansion in Nottingham. The 4th Duke of Newcastle demolished the hall in 1831 to make way for new buildings on Pelham Street. Thurland Street was laid out in 1845, the Corn Exchange built in 1850 and the Thurland Hotel built in 1900 on the site.

Newdigate House
Few seventeenth-century buildings survive, but Newdigate House is an exception. Newdigate House in Castle Gate probably dates from 1675 and is named after the Newdigate family who acquired it in 1714. The house is therefore of the same age as the ducal mansion. There is a marked contrast between the classical façade and the shaped gables of a former period, as exemplified in the small house adjoining with its air of faded continental glory, as shown in our photograph. When Maid Marion Way was constructed in the late 1950s, creating a barrier between the city centre and the castle, these houses were demolished. Fortunately, Newdigate House beyond was not. It became famous as Marshal Tallard's house. In 1704, the Duke of Marlborough defeated the French Forces under Marshal Tallard at the Battle of Blenheim. The marshal was brought to Nottingham and put on parole at Newdigate House where he was to stay from 1705–11. The Marshal seems to have occupied his time there very pleasantly. He designed the flower beds and grew vegetables with new methods, which culminated in writing a book on gardening entitled *Plan du Jardine*. In 1706, an English version was produced entitled *The Retired Gardener*. He also wrote a cookery book, is credited with building two houses in Market Place and organizing boxing and wrestling matches.

A new industry in Nottingham in this period was glassmaking. Glass windows were rare in the Middle Ages, but they became common in the seventeenth century. So did

Newdigate House.

brick houses. In the 1600s, many of the houses in Nottingham were rebuilt in brick with tiled roofs and glass windows. By the early eighteenth century, it was an elegant town with many fine buildings.

Smith's Banking

Thomas Smith (1631–99) was a mercer and local alderman. As with many merchants, his trade led to the safe-keeping of funds and hence to banking. There is no actual record of when he started banking (it was probably earlier in the decade), but Thomas Smith purchased premises in Nottingham Market Square for his merchant and banking business in 1658, so this has been recorded as the year the bank was formed. Regardless of the actual date, Thomas was clearly a banking pioneer and Smith's Bank in Nottingham is believed to have been the first outside London. That would make it the only English provincial bank in the seventeenth century and the oldest existing county bank in England.

Funds came from both the original mercer trade and the collection of excise funds – Thomas had been appointed a sub-commissioner of excise in 1674. The early banking obviously helped Nottingham develop as people were able to take out loans to build and develop businesses.

On the death of Thomas Snr in 1699, Thomas Smith Jnr (1682–1727) succeeded to the business. It was only then that the bank was separated from the original mercer trade. As the bank grew, many firms from as far away as Leeds or Manchester came to Nottingham for banking business. Thomas Smith Jnr had left the bank to his brothers Samuel and Abel. Samuel was a London goldsmith and acted as the London agent, while Abel ran the Nottingham Bank then known as Samuel and Abel Smith & Co. There followed a series of banking partnerships in London and the provinces, all controlled by the Smith family, substantially increasing the scale of the enterprise. In 1902, it merged with the Union Bank of London forming the Union of London & Smith's Bank, which in turn was acquired by the National Provincial Bank in 1918.

At the end of the seventeenth century, the travel writer Celia Fiennes said, 'The town of Nottingham is the neatest town I have seen. It is built of stone and has delicate large and long streets much like London and the houses are lofty and well built. The Market Place is very broad - out of which run two very large streets.'

Nottingham and the Glorious Revolution

Constitutionally, the Civil War established the precedent that an English monarch cannot govern without Parliament's consent, although this concept was legally established only as part of the Glorious Revolution in 1688. After the Civil War and a short period under Oliver Cromwell, the monarchy was restored with Charles II, but when he died without any legitimate children his brother James II was next in line to the throne. However, his Catholicism was unpopular in England and James' eldest daughter, Mary, and her Dutch husband, William of Orange, who were both Protestants, were considered more suitable to rule England instead.

One person that played a major role in this was the Bishop of London, Henry Compton, who was the appointed spiritual adviser to James' daughters, Princess Mary and Princess Anne. Compton travelled to many places including Nottinghamshire, and spoke to countless English peers encouraging their support for William and Mary's intervention. Compton helped to coordinate the arrangements for the rising at Nottingham by conferring with the Earl of Devonshire (made Duke in 1692), the Earl of Stamford, Lord Howe, Lord Delemere and other noblemen and gentry of Nottinghamshire. They met at various alehouses, the most prominent being the Feather's Inn that stood at the corner of Fryer Lane and Wheeler Gate on the spot where the town hall of the French borough formerly stood. The Feathers Inn in turn was replaced by a private house – the predecessor of the modern structure that now occupies the site and is used for business purposes.

It was stressed that Nottingham had an important role to play in securing the crossing of the River Trent should northern factions decide to march to London in support of James. The next day being Saturday, a full market was taking place in Nottingham when Lord Delemere, the Earl of Devonshire, the Earl of Stamford and Lord Howe addressed the crowd at the Malt Cross in Nottingham's Market Square. They informed the people of the danger their religion and liberty were in under the arbitrary proceedings of the King, and that providence had sent his highness, William of Orange, to deliver them from popery and slavery and give them a free parliament. Their speeches were followed by shouts of support from the multitude.

William sailed across the English Channel, arrived at Torbay on 5 November 1688 and marched to London. Princess Anne was in favour of her sister Mary and her husband William taking the throne, but King James was furious. On 24 November, he issued orders to place Princess Anne under house arrest, but desperate to retain her freedom and leave London Anne turned to Bishop Compton, her old tutor, for assistance. The bishop immediately engineered a plan for her escape. Accompanied by several ladies of distinction, the bishop wearing military attire and brandishing a pistol, along with the Earl of Dorset and forty horsemen, Anne was escorted out of London. They subsequently arrived at Nottingham on 1 December where she was very hospitably entertained at the newly built ducal palace by the 2nd Duke.

Princess Anne in Nottingham

Anne had married Prince George of Denmark on 28 July 1683 and within months of the marriage she was pregnant. However, the baby was stillborn in May. Anne recovered at the spa town of Tunbridge Wells where the water is believed to have strong medicinal qualities. When she discovered that she was pregnant again, legend says that as a thank you she presented the town with the pantiles. Over the next two years, Ann gave birth to two daughters in quick succession (Mary and Anne Sophia), but tragedy was about to strike. In early 1687, within a matter of days, Anne miscarried, her husband caught smallpox and their two young daughters died of the same infection. Later that year, Anne suffered another stillbirth, possibly due to the infection. Anne experienced another miscarriage in April 1688 and left London to recuperate in the spa town of Bath. Seven months later, her brother-in-law William arrived in England to take the English throne. Anne left London and arrived in Nottingham.

St Ann's Well

The main road running through the Nottingham district of St Ann's is named Wells Road because until a few centuries ago, a great many natural springs gushed up from the ground along this valley. At the bottom of Ransom Road was Rag Well. The water here was credited with curing eye complaints. The name came from the practice of soaking a rag in the water, bathing the eyes, then hanging the rag on a bush to dry. It's not clear whether this was part of the cure, i.e. as the water in the rag dried the problem eased, or the rag was a communal cloth guaranteed to spread infection through the area.

The principle well in the area was originally known as Oswell or Owswell, which has led to speculation that it could be derived from Robert Fitz Othe, the Earl of Huntingdon who is believed by many to be Robin Hood. It was known as Robin Hood's Well for many centuries.

The earliest information we have about Owswell is that it was linked to a hermitage, so it was considered a holy well due to the healing properties of the water. King Henry IV (1399–1413), who frequently visited Nottingham, is known to have taken the waters at Owswell as a viable cure for his leprosy. In 1409, he gave money to the monks of the hermitage for a chapel to be built and dedicated to St Ann, the patron saint of wells, springs and married women. Tradition says St Ann was mother of the Virgin Mary.

Around 1543, after the Dissolution of the Monasteries, the hermitage and chapel were adapted by the corporation for secular use. In 1617, the hermitage and chapel were replaced by a house of refreshment on a lavish scale. During the seventeenth century, it became the practice for the mayor, aldermen, local dignitaries and other town officials accompanied by their retinue to parade here on Easter Monday. These social outings with lavish entertainment continued until the Civil War when such pomp and ceremony was frowned upon.

During the seventeenth and eighteenth centuries, St Ann's Well was one of the most popular tourist attractions. While staying in Nottingham in 1688 Princess Anne regularly visited the well to take the waters. At the time many believed that the waters helped women conceive. She had been pregnant six times in five years and was desperate for an heir. She had taken the curative waters at Tunbridge Wells and Bath, so understandably she was going to take the waters of St Ann's Well.

Because of her patronage, and the fact that after six pregnancies she still had no children, when it was announced that she was pregnant shortly after her visit to Nottingham it was widely acclaimed that it was due to the health-giving waters of St Ann's Well. When Princess Anne gave birth to a healthy son on 24 July 1689, there was much rejoicing and understandably the connection between the birth of a healthy baby and taking the waters at St Ann's Well was made.

The curative waters attracted huge support. The water that had previously risen into a little pool and flowed away into a stream was now covered by a dome-like structure, designed by Mr Tarbottom, a local architect. In 1797, John Throudy described the well as 'under an arched stone roof … and steps leading down into the water'. This would

The water used to rise into a little pool and form a small stream. Painting by G. Hodgson.

St Ann's Well covered with an ornamental Gothic well house.

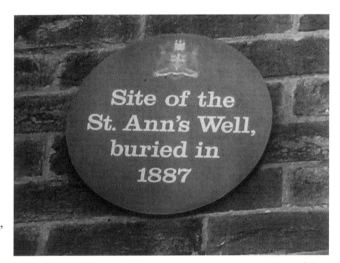

The only sign of St Ann's Well, now in the garden of The Gardner's Inn, Well Road.

indicate that the water, described as 'so cold it would kill a toad', was not only drunk but used for bathing.

St Ann's Well had lost its appeal by the mid-nineteenth century. On 19 November 1855, the town council voted to have the spring bricked up and the buildings demolished to prevent access to the water. The Gothic well-house remained, but only for a further thirty years. In 1887, the Tarbottom structure was demolished when the Great Northern Railway was built and the site was excavated to a depth of 30 feet for the foundations of the north abutment of the rail bridge. The railway offered to present the monument to the town for erection elsewhere, but their offer was refused by the council. The monument, instead of preserving a site of great antiquity, suffered the same sad fate.

The well's location was lost for many years. With the closure of the railway line in 1987, it was located at the rear of the Gardeners public house in Well Road where a plaque was mounted on the side of the building proclaiming that this was the site of St Ann's Well, buried one hundred years previously.

The Royal Children

Princess Anne left Nottingham with her retinue strengthened by 200 of the Duke of Devonshire's troops. She arrived at Oxford on 19 December and returned to London as James II fled to France on the 23 December. In January 1689, a Convention Parliament declared that James had abdicated. William and Mary were declared joint monarchs. This became known as the Glorious Revolution.

The Bill of Rights 1689 and Claim of Rights Act 1689 settled the succession. As William and Mary had no children, Mary's younger sister, Anne, and her descendants were to be next in line. This seemed even more sound when on 24 July 1689, Anne gave birth to a son, Prince William, Duke of Gloucester, at Hampton Court Palace. There was much rejoicing. At last she had a child, a son who would eventually inherit the English Crown.

It was understandable that the connection between the birth of a healthy baby and taking the waters at St Ann's Well was made. Princess Anne's popularity in Nottingham was such that she became the toast of the whole neighbourhood. As a show of royal support, it is thought that the inn on Castle Gate was given its unusual name – The Royal Children. It's been stated wrongly that it was because Princess Anne's children stayed there. Prince William, her only child, wasn't born until eight months after Anne's visit to Nottingham. After Queen Mary's death in 1694, her husband, King William, continued as sole monarch. Princess Anne had a string of miscarriages and stillbirths, then, on 30 July 1700, Prince William died at Windsor Castle. He was just eleven years old and the country went into mourning. When King William died in 1702 he was succeeded by Anne. She had seventeen pregnancies and no heir to the throne. When Anne died, she was the last monarch of the House of Stuart.

The seventeenth-century inn, the Royal Children, at the corner of Castle Gate and St Nicholas Street was demolished in 1933 and replaced with a mock-Tudor replacement of the same name.

9

CAVES

Running for 2 or 3 miles from east to west of Nottingham, there is a sandstone ridge that terminates southwards in cliff faces, representing the north limit of the Trent Valley. It can be divided into the three main sections – Castle Rock, Town Cliff and Sneinton Hermitage. It varies in height from a few feet to 130 feet, and has been excavated throughout its entire length. It was probably in these cliff faces that the earliest excavations were scooped as dwelling places by primitive man.

The earliest and the most important annotation we have are the words of the Welsh monk Asser, Bishop of Sherbourne and friend and biographer of Alfred the Great. Asser visited around AD 900 and gave Nottingham the Welsh name *Tig guocobauc*, meaning 'the dwelling of caves'. This old Welsh form appears in modern Welsh as *ty gogofawg*, meaning 'cave house'.

This would indicate that rock excavations existed in Nottingham long before the Norman Conquest, but because the sandstone is so soft and perishable no form of early ornamentation would have survived over 1,000 years, even under the most favourable conditions. Also, the uninterrupted occupation or utilisation of these places has required them to be refashioned and changed in accordance with need.

In the Domesday Book, one entry states: 'In the ditch of the borough are seventeen houses, and other six houses.' This would refer to the old borough's defence ditch – earthworks built for fortification. The ditch would have been cut out of the sandstone, but by 1086 it presented a face that was apparently no longer in use for defensive purposes. Modern excavations have proved conclusively that the sides of the ditch were so utilised. A rock dwelling was found when Old Queen Street was rebuilt with a central column, door and window. Probably this was in the ancient town ditch, which from its nature and position was always dry. A ditch-dwelling was found in Warser Gate. According to the report, it faced north and had two windows with a door in the middle. A little wall of rock, some 4 feet high, separated it from the primitive ditch.

The discovery of Roman amphoria, or earthenware storage vessels with pointed bottoms, lends weight to the suggestion that the earthworks themselves extend back to ancient times. Some of the oldest caves in the city have revealed pottery dating to between 1270–1300. The Rock Houses on Castle Boulevard have been assigned to all sorts of ages and to all sorts of uses. In Norman times they were the place of residence

The rock dwellings in old Queen Street.

of a religious body who were so important and firmly established that when William Peveril diverted the course of the River Leen to bring it along the foot of the cliff of Nottingham Park, he was obliged to twist its course so as not to disturb these hermits. Throughout the Middle Ages, we know that they were spoken of as the Chapel of St Mary in the Rocks.

Thevisa's translation of Higden's version in his *Polycronicon* (the great history book of the fourteenth and fifteenth century) is quaint:

> Notyngham stondith uppon Trent, and sometyme heet [hight] Snotyngham, that is 'the woning [dwelling] of dennes' [caves], for the Danes dwellid there sometyme, and were i-loggedf as me telleth, and i-digged dennes and caves under hard rokkes and stones.

T. C. Hine of Nottingham quotes an old manuscript published in 1609:

> The whole town is in a manner undermined with caves of an amazing depth and extent, that it is even questioned whether all the buildings on the surface of the rock would fill up the vacancies underneath.' He makes the further comment that – 'when the question of Sunday recreation was discussed in Parliament in the 17th century, one of the members for the borough, stated that as most of his constituents lived underground, he thought they at least were entitled to enjoy themselves in the open air on Sunday.

Around 1620, Richard Corbet, poet and afterwards Bishop of Oxford and Norwich, recorded details of a northern tour and his impression of Nottingham in this rather charming ode.

> Nottingham we next arrived
> Built on a rock, but ill-contrived
> Where we observed the cunning men like moles

Dwell not in houses, but were earthed in holes
So did they not build upwards, but dig through
As hermits' caves, or conies do their borough
Great underminers sure as anywhere
'Tis thought the powder-traitors practised there
Would you not think that men stood on their heads
When gardens cover houses there, like leads
And on the chimneys top the maid may know
Whether her pottage boil, or not, below
There cast in herbs, or salt, or bread, her meat
Contented rather with the smoke than heat
This was the rocky parish, higher stood
Churches and houses, buildings, stone and wood.

John Taylor (1578–1653) was an English poet and waterman who dubbed himself the Water Poet. In 1618, he had published *The Pennylesse Pilgrimage; or, the Moneylesse Perambulation of John Taylor, alias the Kings Magesties Water-Poet; How he travelled on foot from London to Edinborough in Scotland, not carrying any money, neither begging, borrowing, or asking meate, drinke, or lodging.* The time John Taylor spent in Nottingham must have made a great contribution to the book's theme as he wrote:

A great many of the inhabitants, especially the poorer sort, dwell in vaults, holes, or caves, which are digged out of the rock, so that if a man be destitute of a house, he has only to go to Nottingham with a mattock, a shovel, a crow of iron, a chisel, a mallet, and with such instruments he may play the mole, the coney, or pioneer, and work himself a hole and a burrow for himself and his family, where over their heads the grass and pasture grows, beasts do feed, and cows are milked.

Taylor's description would have enticed many to dig themselves a desirable residence (des res), but it was a bit fanciful. It did not apply to Nottingham town where the whole area was in private ownership and where there were no pastures overhead. It might have applied to the cliffs and wastes on the roadsides outside the town, but the town authorities would not be at all pleased with Taylor's pronouncement. It was likely to attract vagabonds and roving inhabitants, who would squat uninvited on the outskirts of the borough spreading epidemic, diseases and otherwise rendering themselves a continual source of trouble and anxiety to the municipality.

The following interesting paragraph is extracted from Woodward's *Eccentric Excursions*, 1796:

The rocks on which the town is built, from the various rude formations of dwellings in the cavities fashioned into chimneys, windows, and other conveniences, were undoubtedly originally inhabited by the ancient Britons. Many of the modern houses are so situated that the inhabitants literally go down stairs to their garrets and upstairs to their gardens. From the walls of the latter the eye of the spectator is frequently

A rock house.

directed to a crowded street at a great depth beneath him. It is scarcely possible to dig a foundation for a house without meeting with subterraneous passages, which are in general used as cellars, some of which have a descent of 40 or 50 steps, and others much deeper. The most remarkable are those of the White Lion and Blackmoor Head Inns, which are usually visited by travellers, if possessed of any curiosity. In the former is a large reservoir for keeping fish alive, for which article the town is much famed, particularly for its salmon taken in the Trent.

The Caves and Passages in Castle Rock

The rock-cut passages and caves under Nottingham Castle appear to have been extensive and numerous and, like the castle itself, practically indestructible. No details have been preserved. On 14 July 1953, the *Nottingham Guardian* revealed that a radium and radon extraction plant had been stored in the caves since the war. It was removed to the radio chemical centre at Amersham. Another section of the caves under the castle are still in regular use as the indoor rifle range of the Nottingham Rifle Club.

One of the most famous passages is the previously mentioned Mortimer's Hole, in its course tapping the south end of the eastern ditch and what may be distinguished as the western sallyport. At least one authority believes that Mortimer's Hole, a direct means of communication with the water at the foot of the rock, was in existence prior to the Conquest and dates to Anglo-Saxon or Danish times. Numerous prisoners have languished in Nottingham's castle dungeons, but the most famous was King David of Scotland, so understandably his place of imprisonment is of interest.

John Leland, an English antiquarian who visited Nottingham around the year 1540, left this early account on record:

There is also a cochlea (a spiral shaped cavity) with a turret over it wher the kepers of the castelle say Edwarde the thirdes band cam up through the rok and toke the Erle Mortymer prisoner. Ther is yet a fair staire to go downe by the rok to the ripe of Line. There be diverse buildinges betwyxt the dungeon and the ynner court of the castelle; and ther goith also doune a stair ynto the grounde, wher Davy kinge of Scottes as the castellanes say, was kept as a prisoner.

In the letterpress accompanying Speed's 1610 map of Nottingham, we read:

Many strange vaults hewed out of the rocks, in this towne are seene; those under the Castle of an especial note, one for the story of Christ's Passion engraven in the Walls, and cut by the hand of David the second King of Scots, whilst he was therein detained prisoner. Another wherein Lord Mortimer was surprised in the non-age of King Edward the Third, ever since bearing the name of Mortimer's Hole. These have their staires and severall roomes made artificially even out of the Rockes; as also in that hill on which the town stands are dwelling houses with winding staires, windowes, chimneys, and roome above roome, wrought all out of the solid rock.

A Lansdowne manuscript in the British Museum records a visit to Nottingham in the year 1634:

The next morninge we found ourselves in a towne nothing but rocke, which way soever we walked. It is sweetly situated on a hill, within a mile of the brave River Trent. All or most of their cellarage, and many artificial dwellings, are hewen and made out of firm rocke; but more than especially of note, at that famous ruinated castle built by William the Conqueror is Mortimer's Hole, into which we descended from the court of the old castle by 150 stayres, all within one mighty huge rocke, on which the castle is founded. After we had tyrd ourselves with clyming up soe high as those commanding towers, and descending down soe low as we did, into those deepe dismall dark vaults and caves, where the King of Scotts was famished miserably to death, and the hole wherein the Lord Mortimer, Earle of Marsh, was surprised, we came marching fayre and easily to the towne.

Discoveries are still being made. In 1899, when excavating for a new wing to the general hospital, another series of rock passages, one of them over 100 yards in length, were laid open on the westward extension of the castle plateau. The spot is outside the medieval castle but within the town defences. The north end of the main hospital building stands on the site of an ancient mound. When disturbed over a century ago, a dagger and several interments were found. Under this place a winding passage less than 4 feet in height and, consequently, only to be traversed in a stooping posture, led to a well over a 100 feet deep. It would appear as though the mound were anciently capable of defence; self-contained in regard to its water supply and equipped with private sallyports. The primary modern meaning for sallyport is a secure, controlled entryway as of a fortification or a prison that is usually protected by some means.

Pen Pits and Rock Hewn Dungeons

In medieval times, the castle caves were used as primitive, rock-hewn dungeons, but there were other buildings in the town equipped with primitive, deep dungeons too. The King's Hall of the County on High Pavement and its near neighbour, the old town hall at Weekday Cross, had both been courts of justice from early times. Countless unfortunate humans would have been taken from here to execution on Gallows Hill or thrown in the dungeons below to languish and die. When St John's poorhouse and house of correction was set up in *c.* 1600, it also had dungeons below ground. As all three places were visited and described by Howard the philanthropist, towards the close of the eighteenth century, we know these places were still in use long after then.

When the course of the Great Central Railway was being excavated, many previously unrecorded, curiously shaped funnel or bell-shaped holes were laid bare. Because their dates and origins were unknown, they were tentatively called pen-pits. If these dated back to primitive man, they could have served as pitfalls for man or wild beast and as houses of detention for either. They were most in evidence on the site of the old town hall, which would suggest that they served as prisons or dungeons.

The late James Shipman F.G.S (Fellow of the Geological Society of London), recorded them and described them as such:

> Probably the oldest of them (the Town Hall caverns) – certainly the most remarkable
> – was a series of bell-shaped holes made in the highest part of the ground, and within

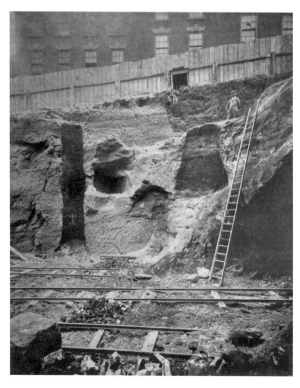

Excavating for the railway revealed many wells and pits.

the precincts of the old Town Hall. In fact, two, if not three, were found underneath the building itself, and two others under the prison yard at the back. The conical holes were hollowed out of a platform of sandstone eight or ten feet below the level of Weekday-cross but had been filled up at some time or other, apparently in the latter part of the eighteenth century, judging by the character of the pottery they contained. They were filled with dark soil, coal slack, half-burnt cinders, bits of charcoal, and yellow sand, sometimes in layers.

They were not confined to the site of the old Town Hall. Two more of these curious conical excavations were found at the corner of Fletcher-gate and Weekday-cross, and about 60ft. back from the roadway. The deepest and most conspicuous of them was found at the north-east angle of the cutting at Weekday-cross, and just at the mouth of the tunnel. This was circular in shape. It was 16ft 7in in depth, and 7ft 6in in diameter at the bottom, narrowing towards the top to 4ft. The bottom of the hole was not flat, as was the case with the rest of these holes, but was curiously concave, the centre being as much as 15 inches lower than the circumference. The bottom of the hole was two feet above the level of the railway. There were indications that the hole had been rudely arched over with lumps of sandrock, cemented together and covered over with concrete, at some period, probably when the hole was filled up. The old massive stone wall of the cells passed over the eastern edge of it, the hole itself being immediately under the floor of the cell.

The second cone-shaped cavity was on the opposite side of the railway cutting. This hole was not circular, but was nearly square, the sides converging in wards towards the

The bell-shaped hole where iron shackles were found.

top, so that, although it was 7ft wide at the bottom, it was only 4ft 6in wide at the top, and was 11ft. deep. The bottom was 9ft above the base of the cutting. In the circular pit there was no indication as to how it was entered, and no trace whatever of steps; but in this one there were traces of foot-holes on one side at least, the other side having been cut away before the cavity was discovered. The third of those curious cavities was met with at the extreme southern edge of the gaol precincts, on the east side of the cutting, and about 54ft from the deep, circular pit. It was, in fact, just underneath the back wall of the prison yard. Like the second one described, it was more or less square in shape, but one side was perpendicular, while the other sides overhung. The hole was 10ft deep and 7ft at the bottom, narrowing to about 4ft at the top.

Mr Shipman then goes on to speak of three other such holes found in the same neighbourhood. Coming to the question of their original purpose, he truthfully says none of the local historians allude to anything like them, concluding:

I have learnt that in the bell-shaped hole at the north-west corner of the Weekday-cross cutting, about a foot from the bottom, iron shackles for securing the legs of a prisoner were found. Embedded in the side of the hole was an eye-bolt, or staple, with a piece of chain attached, by which the prisoners had been secured. The irons were completely corroded with trust, go much so, in fact, that they were regarded as useless, and not worth preserving, and they were thrown away. This removes all doubt as to what these holes found underneath the old Town Hall were used for, at one time at any rate. At a later period they were probably used as refuse pits, and were finally completely filled up and covered over.

10

THE TOWN OF CAVE DWELLINGS

Underneath the streets, houses, shops and offices of Nottingham lie a labyrinth of passages linking hundreds of caves that have been in use for over 1,000 years. Nottingham has more manmade caves than anywhere else in Britain. Each cave is unique and it's doubtful that any were formed naturally. They were all cut into the sandstone by the city's inhabitants for use as hermitages, churches, hiding places, isolation hospitals, houses, cellars and places of work.

The need for clean water and subsequent creation of wells were the most common motive for burrowing. The following is the abstract of an interesting Latin charter dated 1469/70:

> Licence from Thomas Thurland, of Nottingham, to Alice, who was the wife of John Lyversege, her heirs or assigns, residing and commorant in her tenement in the holding of William Hurst, smith, upon the Longrawe ... to draw and take water from and in a well of the said Thomas Thurland, dusr out of the rock in his underground cellar belonging to his aforesaid tenement, with licence for the said Alice and her assigns to come, during the time of their residence there, upon the land of the tenement aforesaid with their vessels so often as it shall be necessary, and to draw and carry away water to her own land; providing that the aforesaid Alice or her assigns residing in the tenement aforesaid shall contribute to the repairing of the well aforesaid and of the buckets and ropes and other fittings.

Bugholes or Isolation Hospital

In 1503/04 there is a reference to Bugholes. It's not certain whether the name was derived from the Bugge family whose mansion from around the early thirteenth century occupied a site above them in Castle Gate, or from the bog or marsh that the caves faced. In accounts that have survived from 1543/44, there is a reference to the pool yard beneath the 'Boke Holles'. Even more enlightening is the fact that the sum of 2s was paid out 'at the commandementes of Master Mayre for the vyset folke in Boge Holys' to one Thomas Guymer. Could the 'vyset folke' be the 'visited' or plague-stricken townspeople? If so, the bugholes were then being utilised for housing plague victims, and as such, they were the earliest local isolation hospitals on record. They could also have served as the oldest leper hospitals in use long before 1543.

Thomas Guymer was probably either a keeper or a constable. Fourteen years later, we find him collecting the toll of salt in the public market.

How Big Are the Caves?
Deering, the first Nottingham historian writing around 1745, disclosed,

> structures of a very considerable extent, arched in a regular manner, and supported by columns with carved capitals, &c., framed for places of worship, hewn out of the rook, have been discovered by workmen when digging for foundations, with very obscure entrances, hardly to be suspected, and also other apartments for lodging-places. Such were observed under divers houses on the Row, on the south side of the Great Market-place, called Timber Hill, and one Edward Goddard, a bricklayer yet living, assures me that when he was an apprentice, being at work on the east side of the Weekday-cross, he there got into one of these subterranean fabrics, which he found supported and adorned with pillars, as has been mentioned, and that he made his way from one spacious place to another, till he came as far as the upper end of Pilcher-gate and under a small close at present the property of John Sherwin, Esq., and opposite to his dwelling-house. He, the said Goddard, says that in one of these places he found a wooden cup and a wooden can, which seemed to be sound and whole, but that when he took hold of them they mouldered into dust.

Carvings in the Caves
In 1865, Alderman Thomas Herbert had a house built on the Ropewalk, then called Victoria Street, north of The Park. To gain access to his garden on the slope overlooking The Park on the other side of the road, he had a flight of steps and a tunnel driven

A labyrinth of passages link hundreds of caves under Nottingham.

through the solid rock underneath the roadway. When the sides of this subterranean passage were being carved, the workmen broke through into other caves on the terraces overlooking The Park. Thomas and his cousin, William Herbert, had one of these caves made into a conservatory. Into this he inserted coloured windows to throw tinted lights on the weird beasts he had carved in the rock to look as if they were lurking among the plants. Another cave was made into an Egyptian temple with carvings of Druids, Sphinxes and other strange creatures designed to overawe the spectator. In a third grotto he had a biblical theme: Daniel in the Lion's Den, with lifesize figures of Daniel and the lions – an impressive spectacle.

The Nottingham Sandmen

Although Thomas Herbert's digging started as a convenience, it became a work of art, but most digging was for a far more utilitarian purpose. In 1815, Blackner, a Nottingham historian, wrote about Rouse's Cavern – the largest of the old rock habitations that lined Mansfield Road. It ran under Dog Kennel Hill and Peel Street on the west side of the road leading from St Mary's Workhouse to Gallows Hill. This wasn't just the home of James Rouse who had given the cave his name; it gave him his livelihood too. James Rouse was a sandman who went round the Nottingham streets calling 'Lily white sand-o; who wants some lily white sand-o?' Sand had been mined for centuries for road mending, spreading on floors and as an abrasive cleaner, and during a period of thirty years James Rouse worked in and took away the sand from the cave, bag by bag on the back of his ass to sell to the housewives of the town and neighbourhood to scatter on their floors. He retired to St Nicholas' Workhouse where he died in 1810.

People had been earning a living selling the sand door-to-door in the same manner as Rouse for centuries, then in 1811, the year after James Rouse died, the decision was made to fill the caves in. Distressed mechanics and artisans of the town were employed to do the work by the overseers of St Mary's parish, rather than take them

Caves in the church cemetery.

and their families into the workhouse. The area, as already stated, was between St Mary's Workhouse and Gallows Hill in the area of Church Cemetery, so it was no great surprise when over thirty human skeletons were found.

To appreciate the size of these caves, there's an old story that certain men were lost for a day and a night in the huge caves, which still exist underneath Mansfield Road and Sherwood Street.

The area was still making headlines twenty years later when the local directory of 1832 stated:

> Many rock-houses within the limits of the town of Nottingham are still inhabited, though a considerable number have of late years been destroyed by the Corporation, and the sites let on building leases. A long range of these singular dwellings are now in ruins on the east side of Mansfield Road, where they were broken up a few years ago. The Corporation were prevented from building the projected row of brick houses on the site to correspond with those on the opposite side of the road, by the cupidity of the sturdy troglodyte Samuel Caulton, a super-animated smith. He and his wife inhabit the uppermost house in the rock, opposite to which he has erected a blacksmith's shop. Having many years occupied the place without paying any acknowledgment, he now claims it as his own freehold property, and consequently refused to budge when the Corporation officers ejected his neighbours.

Samuel Caulton's perversity obviously paid off as he and his wife were allowed to remain there until their deaths.

Demolition of the Sneinton Hermitage rock houses, 1897.

Sneinton Hermitage

In a rental of 1544, we first read of Sneinton Hermitage: 'Item, there is a hous under the grounde in a roche of stone that somtyme was called the hermitage.'

In a later rental dated 1591, we read: 'The Ermytage in Sneynton, being a house cutte oute of rock, and paieth yearly 2s.' It is likely that these entries refer to a particular cave, or range of caves, probably with land attached, which had been a medieval hermitage occupied by members of a reclusive religious order, but was then disused as such. Its name was subsequently absorbed by the whole line of dwellings built into the length of the 300-m Bunter sandstone ridge that became known as Sneinton Hermitage. The transference of the name from one cavern to an extensive series had the unfortunate effect of causing the original hermitage, which would include a rock-cut chapel, to be lost and it has never been identified in modern times. No doubt many of these dwellings that were dug on waste ground or by roadsides for which no rent was paid did not officially exist because they failed to figure on the town rentals. This was the largest group of cave houses in Nottingham and they were frequently of two stories with carved stone staircases and fireplaces. Windows were glazed, and shelves and storage spaces might be cut into the rock. Many also had their own well.

Sneinton Hermitage is now a continuation of Station Street running east under the A61 and the A612 Manvers Street. When Manvers Road was first constructed, brick buildings were built facing into the sandstone using the caves as back rooms. In 1829, a rock collapse destroyed these buildings. In 1845, the St Mary's Inclosure Act was passed. Inclosure is an old or formal spelling of the word now more usually spelled 'enclosure'. The act enclosed open fields and common land, creating legal property rights to land that was previously considered common. It also banned the renting of cellars and caves as homes for the poor, but some of these caves and others locally were inhabited until 1867.

In 1897, a railway expansion forced Manvers Road to divert, cutting away much of the rock face and erasing most of Sneinton's remaining caves. The last of these were demolished in 1904 as part of a road-widening scheme. Sneinton Hermitage has recently been largely cut away in connection with modern street improvements.

Drury Hill

Drury Hill was a very old thoroughfare and one of the main streets in the Narrow Marsh area of the city. In the Middle Ages, although narrow, it was easier to climb than the track by Malin Hill, Long Stairs and Hollow Stone. The main entrance to the town from the south was along Narrow Marsh and up the much less severe gradient of Drury Hill. This line consequently became the chief business thoroughfare of the town until the seventeenth century. Then wheeled traffic began to come into general use and it was found that this ancient roadway was too narrow to deal with the cumbrous vehicles of the times. The gradient of Hollow Stone was eased, and that was turned into a principal entrance to the town.

Drury Hill, leading from Low Pavement to Sussex Street, was at one time called Vault Lane after Vault Hall that stood at the junction with Low Pavement. Later, it was called Parkyn Lane, probably after some member of the Parkyn family of Bunny. It became Drury Hill around 1620 from one of the leading figures in Nottingham,

Alderman Drury, a wealthy cordwainer who lived at Vault Hall. We'd call him a shoemaker today. Vault Hall, anciently the property of the Plumtre family, got its name in turn from the huge vaults beneath it. In the fourteenth century at the time of the staple, great quantities of wool was lodged in these vaults.

The vaults, along with the caves on Drury Hill, were also used as hiding places by the persecuted flock that had worshipped at St Mary's church in the early days of Nonconformity and during the religious persecutions in the later Stuart period.

Drury Hill and the Garner's Hill

In medieval Nottingham, this area was a wealthy neighbourhood. However, by the nineteenth century, some of the worst slums in Britain could be found here. Housing was in short supply in Nottingham and the poorest families often rented underground spaces where entire families slept, ate and lived in a single room. The overcrowding and poor sanitation made it a breeding ground for diseases such as cholera, tuberculosis and smallpox. Something had to be done about the congestion and the answer seemed to be wholesale development. In 1892, there were thirty-five businesses and three public houses on Drury Hill. When the Great Central Railway viaduct was built across the area in 1896, it necessitated the demolition of many properties.

Broadmarsh and the City of Caves

Broadmarsh was originally the name of the street that went from Lister Gate to Drury Hill, but everything changed when the decision to build the Broadmarsh shopping

Demolition of the property on Garner's Hill, 1896.

centre was taken in the mid-1960s. The Broadmarsh centre stretches from Maid Marion Way on the west to the elevated Middle Hill on the east, and absorbs the area as far south as Canal Street. The new development meant the destruction of the areas many narrow streets and curiously haphazard buildings.

The initial designs for the Broadmarsh centre included filling in all the caves, but once the site was cleared in 1968 the Nottingham Historical Arts Society made a detailed recording of the caves. This showed how important they were. In the past, the peculiar characteristics of these caves made them attractive to craftsmen and traders. Blacksmiths on Bridlesmith Gate used them as workshops, while fishmongers on Fisher Gate and butchers on Goose Gate utilised them as storage. When the only surviving example of a medieval underground tannery was discovered here, plans for the centre were changed and most of the caves were saved.

Recognised as being of national importance and scheduled as an ancient monument, the caves were cleared and, in 1972, the Friends of Nottingham Museum began running guided tours of the caves accessed from the upper mall of the Broadmarsh shopping centre.

Underground Breweries

Caves were particularly popular with maltsters – malting being the process of turning barley into malt, which was one of the city's principle occupations from the thirteenth century onwards. It's one of the first trades that we know to have developed here. Barley was obtained from the Vale of Belvoir and the natural water of Nottingham was rich in gypsum. Combining the two made a winning formula. The consistent temperature in the caves, which were neither cold in winter nor hot in summer, was

The only surviving example of an underground medieval brewery.

ideal for brewing and storing. These subterranean malt rooms had a distinct advantage to year-round brewing. The quality and taste of the mature beer resulted in the fame of Nottingham beer spreading, and great quantities were exported throughout Mercia by our Saxon forefathers. Most public houses used caves to store their ale.

According to Celia Fiennes, it was also served down there. When she visited the town in 1697, she placed on record that 'Nottingham is famous for good ale, also for Cellars. They are all dugg out of the Rocks, and so are very Coole. Att ye Crown Inn is a Cellar of 60 stepps down, all in ye Rock, like arch worke over your head: in ye Cellar I dranke good ale.' The Crown Inn that Celia Fiennes refers to stood on the Long Row and has long since been demolished.

The Underground Tannery

Nottingham's caves can boast Britain's only surviving underground medieval tannery. The Marsh area of the city was renowned for its tanneries, and by 1667, there were forty-seven here. Tanning is the process by which animal skins are preserved and made usable as leather. The process is long, dirty and very smelly, requiring large quantities of dung and urine, which produced a stench so foul as to repel even the rats. In medieval times, leather was used for making shoes, belts, gloves, harnesses, armour and bottles.

The reconstructed tannery now consists of two caverns, which were cut into the cliff face and previously open to a yard where other burning processes were undertaken. There was an opening to the River Leen where they would wash the skins in the town's drinking water.

The oldest is the Pillar Cave, so named for the large column that supports the roof. Both caves had wells, but in this cave a King John groat was found in the well, suggesting that it was in use before 1250. The cave had been buried by a rock fall in around 1400 and reopened as part of the tannery around 1500. The second cave is equal in size and includes a dozen vats lined with clay, which have been cut into the floor to contain the solutions. The size of the vats suggests smaller skins like sheep or goats were being tanned, rather than cowhide.

Air-Raid Shelters

During the Second World War, the people of Nottingham used the caves as air-raid shelters to protect them from the bombs that descended upon the city. Older caves were reopened and made suitable, and new purpose-built air-raid shelter caves were cut into the sandstone. The largest of these new caves was cut underneath Player's factory in Radford and was capable of sheltering 9,000 people. By February 1941, eighty-six caves in Nottingham were available as public shelters. The sandstone caves were also a useful source of sand for sandbags and a number of holes were dug to supply the demand. These caves were once separate caverns but were joined together during the Second World War so that they could be used as air-raid shelters.

11

NOTTINGHAM IN THE EIGHTEENTH CENTURY

Nottingham grew steadily despite outbreaks of plague that occurred throughout the sixteenth and early seventeenth century. The last outbreak was in 1667. By 1600, Nottingham's population was between 3,500 and 4,000, rising to 5,000 by the late seventeenth century. Chapel Gate, the last medieval gate in the city wall, was demolished in 1743 to ease traffic flow. Several narrow streets were widened and new buildings erected.

The Exchange Building
The exchange building dominated the head of the Market Square and was built in 1724 at a cost of £2,400. The architect was Marmaduke Pennel who was also mayor for the year 1724/25. It was largely rebuilt in 1815 to include a council chamber and

The exchange building at the head of the Market Square.

mayor's apartments along with all the many rooms used for public purposes. There was a very large room, often referred to as the ballroom. On the north side of the exchange building with an entrance from Smithy Row was the police office where the magistrates of the town sat every Tuesday and Friday morning to determine what cases should come before them. Underneath the exchange and facing the Market Place were four shops and a public house called The Shambles. The principal part of the ground floor was laid out in extensive shambles and was the butcher's quarters. There was a clock in the gable built by Woolley, but in 1876, a time ball was installed on the roof of the exchange. This was a common device at the time. An electrical impulse from Greenwich at 1.00 p.m. caused the ball to slide down the pole. It probably wasn't very successful as the apparatus was dismantled in 1887/88.

The Nottingham Goose Fair

The Goose Fair first appears in official records in 1541, although it's traditionally dated much earlier. In 1752, the date of the fair was changed because in that year, an Act was passed to reduce the calendar and eleven days were dropped from the month of September. The change meant that what had previously been St Mathew's Day (21 September) became the 2 October. From 1752–1875 that was the opening day of the fair.

In 1764 there was a riot at the fair because cheese cost 8½d a pound. People who had come into the city to lay in food stocks for the winter started an uproar. One man picked up a cheese and hurled it at a stall holder. Stalls were overturned and cheeses were thrown or bowled along the ground. The militia were called in to restore order. On another occasion, in 1831 when the news came that the Reform Bill had been rejected, the mob left the fair to help set light to Nottingham Castle. A committee was set up to investigate the moral, social and commercial aspects of the fair. In 1876, the duration of the fair was reduced from eight days to five. Later it was reduced to three. In the mid-1890s, the fair spread out over the land now covered by King Street and Queen Street and into Wheeler Gate, where one side from South Parade Corner to St Peter's Gate was yet to be built up. In 1891, the show was lighted for the first time by electric light. The fair was suspended during the First World War. It was held for the last time in the Old Market Square in 1927, and the following year it was accommodated on the Forest.

The Lings Racecourse

The area known as the Lings was once part of Sherwood Forest. It was not a dense mass of trees, but a sandy wasteland with scrubby bushes and a few hardy trees. In a primitive state of cultivation for centuries, animals both wild and domestic grazed the area bisected by ancient paths cut by centuries of passing feet.

The Lings were a resource for the people of Nottingham and a centre for sports and shows. Gentlemen and nobility used the Lings to race their horses. The earliest racecourse was 4 miles long shortened in stages over the years to 1 mile. Racing at the Lings ended in 1890, but at one time Nottingham's races ranked alongside those at Newmarket, York and Ascot.

Lings Racecourse.

Green's Windmill

There were twenty-one windmills and thirteen were on or near the forest. It's just possible to see some of them on the skyline on the previous racecourse painting. One of the most unusual was a smock mill, a mill on which the cap only and not the body turned so that the sails were facing the wind. The only one of its kind, it was worked by steam until it was burnt down on 2 December 1858. All the others were post mills and all had living accommodation attached. When the mob rioted and burned down Nottingham Castle, the crowd came to one of the mills of Nottingham Forest, threw the corn and flour into the street and attempted to set fire to the mill.

Green's Windmill, located at the top of Sneinton Hill overlooking the city of Nottingham, is a fully restored tower mill built in 1807 on the site of a previous post mill. At that time, there were at least two other mills on the nearby, aptly named, Windmill Lane.

A tower mill is a brick or stone tower on which sits a wooden 'cap' or roof that can rotate to bring the sails into the wind. This rotating cap on a firm masonry base gave tower mills great advantages over earlier post mills. They could be built much higher and carry larger sails, which were more efficient. The tower mill was an important source of power for nearly 600 years from 1300–1900, contributing to 25 per cent of the industrial power of all wind machines before the advent of the steam engine and coal power. Green's Mill and the accompanying house were built around 1807 by George Green, who worked the mill and lived in the adjacent house with his family. His son, also called George, was the nineteenth-century mathematical physicist who, after the death of his father in 1829, operated the mill until his own death in 1841.

The mill was still in use until the 1860s, after which it was abandoned and gradually fell into disrepair. In 1923, a copper cap was fitted at the top to make the building

Green's restored windmill.

watertight, and this survived until a fire destroyed it in 1947. Standing derelict, it was acquired by Nottingham City Council in 1979. Funds were raised and it was renovated by Thompson's, millwrights of Alford, Lincolnshire in 1984–86. It was reopened on 2 December 1986 and is now part of a science centre that is open to the public.

The Old Theatre Royal

In 1760, the Old Theatre Royal was built on St Mary's Gate by a man called Whitely, who was the proprietor of a stock company that toured theatres in the neighbouring towns. The theatre was used as a concert hall and in 1772 a music festival was held there. The theatre closed in 1837 and almost immediately reopened as a music hall. The Empire Palace of Variety was built in 1898 on the site of the Old Theatre Royal dressing rooms. Variety theatres fell into decline in the 1950s and the Empire closed in 1958. The building was pulled down and in its place was built the Royal Concert Hall, which opened in 1982.

The present Theatre Royal was the brainchild of two lace dressers named John and William Lambert, who commissioned an architect to design a building on Parliament Street opposite the new Market Street that was replacing the former narrow Sheep Lane. The theatre, with its imposing portico and seating for 2,000 people, proved to be a huge success. It opened on 25 September 1865 and 100 years later it was purchased by the city council when it was in danger of closing. Its restoration began in 1977. The character of

The Theatre Royal, 1853.

the Victorian theatre has been retained, but the auditorium has been remodelled and the antiquated dressing rooms and backstage facilities have all been rebuilt.

The Assemblies

Deering, Nottingham's first historian writing about the social life of Nottingham near the middle of the eighteenth century said:

> Two monthly assemblies contrived for the interview of the genteel part of the town of both sexes, where the younger divert themselves with dancing, whilst the senior or graver part enjoy themselves over a game of Quadrille or Whist. One of these places of meeting is on the Low Pavement … This is called the Ladies' Assembly. The other, called the Tradesmen's Assembly, is held in a large room 70 feet long and 20 feet broad, where the wealthy tradesmen, their wives and sons and daughters, meet for this same recreation. This is at Thurland Hall in Gridlesmith Gate. (The former Thurland Hall, later renamed Clare Hall, being by this time opposite the famous Blackamoor's Inn was used by the innkeepers of the Blackamoor's Inn for large dinner parties, and as attorney's chambers. The hall was demolished in 1831). The usual days of these assemblies are – that of the Ladies the first Tuesday, and that of the Tradesmen every third Tuesday in the month, when in the evening there is in both a numerous appearance. In both these places there are held Assemblies extraordinary, in the Assize week, Election time, and at the Horse Races.

Newspapers

The first regular English daily newspaper, the *Daily Courant*, was launched with the reign of Queen Anne in 1702. Nottingham's first newspaper was probably the *Weekly*

Courant, published by William Ayscough in August 1712. It was followed by the *Nottingham Post* in 1716, then in 1723 Ayscough took over the *Nottingham Post*, combined the two and later that year he published the *Nottingham Weekly Courant*. The *Courant* lasted until 1769, when Samuel Cresswell bought it and changed its name to the *Nottingham Journal* in 1787. For over 200 years, the *Nottingham Journal* went through several title changes through mergers, takeovers, acquisitions and ownership changes. In 1887, the *Nottingham Journal* was incorporated in the *Nottingham Daily Express*. Other titles have come and gone. The *Nottingham Evening Post* began publication in 1878 and now remains the only daily paper printed by the Nottingham Post Group. The *Nottingham Journal* merged with the *Nottingham Guardian* in 1953 forming the *Guardian Journal*. The *Nottingham Evening News* amalgamated with the *Nottingham Evening Post* in 1963.

The celebrated children's author J. M. Barrie (Sir James Matthew, Baronet Barrie, 1860–1937) worked as a staff reporter at the *Nottingham Journal* from 1883 to 1884 at 3 guineas a week. This is where he began his career in journalism, handwriting daily leaders and Monday columns under the pseudonym Hippomenes, along with whimsical Thursday essays attributed to 'A Modern Peripatetic'. He lived in the area known as the Arboretum and it's rumoured that his great story *Peter Pan* was inspired by a Nottingham street urchin he saw walking in Clifton Grove. There's a plaque at the *Nottingham Journal* offices to mark J. M. Barrie's employment there.

The writer Graham Greene (1904–91) was a sub-editor on the *Nottingham Journal* before launching his career as a novelist. By 1943, he was described as being the leading English male novelist of his generation. Most of his novels and many of his plays and short stories have now been adapted for film or television.

Water

Initially, Nottingham people obtained their water from wells or from the rivers. River water was distributed by carriers known as higglers. In 1696, the original waterworks obtained a lease from the Corporation and built pumps driven by a waterwheel at the bottom of Finkhill Street/Canal Street. The pumps took water from the River Leen and forced it into a small reservoir on the east side of Park Row, just above Postern Street. From this, pipes of all sizes led to most parts of the town. With the population explosion between 1720–1830, the supply from the River Leen became inadequate and contaminated with sewage and industrial waste.

Epidemics of cholera and typhoid occurred and, although the causes were not fully understood, it gradually became recognized that the condition of the water was contributory. In 1830, the waterworks company abandoned the River Leen as their source of supply in favour of purer spring water collected in a reservoir of about 1 acre at Basford. Water from the reservoir was fed by gravity through a 10-inch iron pipe to a new pumping station on the River Leen at the foot of the Castle Rock, from where it was pumped to the reservoir near to the general hospital. The pumps at the Castle Works could be driven either by a waterwheel or a rotative beam engine, each of around 16 HP.

The new Trent Waterworks Co. opened its works at Trent Bridge in 1831. This remarkable system was the first in the country to provide a supply at constant high pressure, preventing contamination from entering the mains. It was constructed under supervision of its designer, the company engineer, Thomas Hawksley, then twenty-five-years-old. Water flowed through brick filter tunnels laid in the gravel beds on the north side of the river into a reservoir adjoining the pumping station. From there it was pumped by a 40-HP rotative beam engine to a new reservoir built on the corner of Park Row and the Ropewalk. Parts of this 15-inch, cast-iron water main between the pumping station and the reservoir remain in service today.

Whale Oil Lighting

A couple of hundred years ago, whale oil was very much in demand and supplanted candles for lighting. This made the whale fisheries of Whitby and the other north-east ports very prosperous. The oil was brought to Nottingham in bulk and the innkeepers, keen to use this improved means of lighting their establishments, would act as wholesalers and sell to householders. That's why the shoulder blade of a whale used to be on display above the entrance of the Royal Children Inn. This whale bone would no doubt have been acquired from a whaling skipper as a form of advertisement to be hung above the door. The original old inn on the site had the name painted on this shoulder blade. When the old inn was demolished and the present building erected, this whalebone was hung over the door but it's now inside in a glass case for protection.

The earliest record of any attempt at street lighting in England occured in Charles I's reign when a patent was granted to hang out a lantern in front of every twelfth house in London. Nottingham remained in gloom until 1762 when the Corporation of Nottingham took powers for public lighting and festooned the streets, at somewhat rare intervals, with lamps and lamp holders similar to those remaining on the palings of St Mary's churchyard. These two wrought-iron lamp holders are all that is left of the street lighting of ancient Nottingham. A great globe of thick glass was fixed in each of the iron circles, and this glass was filled with whale oil upon which floated a wick that was lighted. Because the palings round St Mary's church were only set up in 1807, we may assume that these lamp holders date from that time too.

The supply of whale oil for the town was kept in casks under the steps leading up to the old Guild Hall in Weekday Cross and the smell from this stock must have rendered the neighbourhood somewhat unpleasant.

Gas-Lighting the Town

In 1814, gas was first introduced into Nottingham as a public illuminant and, on 8 May 1818, after various Nottingham townsmen collaborated to get a bill passed in Parliament, the Nottingham Gas Light & Coke Co. was established. The first works was erected at Butchers Close at the bottom of Hollow Stone beside the Nottingham Canal. The plant was probably designed by Thomas Livesey. It was decided that ten lamps were quite sufficient to illuminate the whole town. One lamp was set up at the top of Hollow Stone, another at the top of Drury Hill, three in front of the exchange and five in Bridlesmith Gate. At this time Bridlesmith Gate underwent a number of changes. Flagstone footpaths were laid instead of boulders and the roadway was newly opened. With the introduction of gaslights, the street took on a new appearance and an effort was made to change the name to Bond Street, but that proved unsuccessful.

On 14 April 1819, the city streets were lit by gas for the first time. Crowds flocked to witness the miracle of a flame burning without a wick, but fascination was mixed with fear in case the pipes conveying the gas to the burners should explode and blow them all up. Increased demand led to a second holder at Butchers Close in the early 1820s, and by 1835 this had increased to five.

The Nottingham Gas Act 1842 extended the limits of supply to outlying areas of the city. Over the next thirty years, the company expanded with new works built at Radford in 1844 and Basford in 1854. The Nottingham Corporation Gas Act 1874 transferred the company to local authority control at a meeting on 1 May 1874 when a meeting of shareholders at the George Hotel approved the transfer of ownership. The accepted offer was a payment of £75 for each £50 share. The Nottingham Corporation Gas office was based on George Street, adjoining the George Hotel.

By 1914, 7 million cubic feet of gas was made daily from 700 tons of coal and by 1936 Radford had become a reserve station. Following Nationalisation in 1949, the Nottingham Corporation Gas Co. became part of the Nottingham and Derby division of the East Midlands Gas Board, then the British Gas Corporation in 1972.

12

THE HOSIERY AND LACE TRADE

Wool had been woven and felted in the county for centuries, although the introduction of knitting in England is controversial. Henry VIII wore cloth hose, then his son Edward received a pair of knitted silk hose from Spain. According to the King's household accounts, on 7 September 1533 he 'peyd for 4 peyr of knytt hose = viii' s'. A further payment on 3 October 1538 was made for 'two peyr of knytt hose = i' s'. If this can be translated as four pairs for 8s, making them 2s a pair, why had the price fallen to two pairs for 1s? Could this be because the first consignment was made in Spain, the second made in England and knitted hose were becoming very popular?

This would appear to be the first mention of knitted stockings in England and probably started the cottage industry that would change Nottingham. There's an old story that the girlfriend of the Revd William Lee was always knitting when he went round to call. Living in the village of Calverton in Nottinghamshire this would have been a regular form of employment for the villagers. The young lady in question was so occupied with her knitting that the Revd Lee decided to invent a machine that would take over from the hand knitting so that their courtship might progress.

In fact, the ingenious William Lee, Master of Arts of St John's College, Cambridge, devised a machine for knitting stockings in 1589 and laid the foundation for the stocking manufactury of England. Richard Parkyns, MP for Nottingham, arranged for William Lee and his brother to go to London and demonstrated how the machine worked. He wanted royal patronage from Queen Elizabeth, but the Queen was apprehensive. She believed the invention would harm the livelihood of the poor people who obtained their living by knitting, so she refused. The Lees returned to Calverton mortified. However, William persevered in making further improvements to the machine and obtained an introduction to the French Ambassador, who told his Sovereign, Henry IV of France.

The King of France was more impressed than the Queen of England, and invited William Lee over to France with the promise of honours and rewards. William with his family and nine workmen, went and took his machinery to Rouen in Normandy where he worked to the great satisfaction of the King until the monarch was murdered.

William Lee's creditors sold the machinery and stripped him of everything. He died shortly afterward and his workmen returned to England.

Largely due to William Lee's invention, by 1640 silk stockings were being knitted, and from the 1690s the trade knitting silk and wool hosiery boomed. Fifty years later, one third of Nottingham's burgesses were hosiers. By 1739, there were 1,200 stocking frames in the town organised on the domestic or putting out system. Working in their own homes, the normal procedure was for the men to produce the hosiery on the machines and the women and children to hand knit the ribbing that kept the stockings in place. The two parts then had to be sewn together to produce the finished stockings.

Over the years, improvements were made to William Lee's machine and patents taken out by succeeding workers, then, in 1758, came the first major development. Jedediah Strutt added another set of needles to William Lee's machine and produced a rib fabric able to produce hosiery with shape and fit, plus elasticated tops on one machine. This was a breakthrough and Strutt's Derby Rib Machine revolutionised the industry in an age when stockings were an important fashion accessory for men and women.

It was the development of the hosiery trade that gave Nottingham a manufacturing base on which an industrial town was built. By 1812, there were 2,600 stocking frames in Nottingham and this couldn't have happened without the work of three great creators. James Hargreaves is credited with inventing the Spinning Jenny in 1764, Richard Arkwright patented the water frame in 1769 and Samuel Crompton combined the two to create the spinning mule in 1779.

James Hargreaves

James Hargreaves grew up in the town of Blackburn, Lancashire, known for the production of Blackburn greys (cloths with a linen warp, the thread that goes from top to bottom) and cotton weft (the thread that goes from left to right). The one-thread spinning wheel could not keep up with demand, but Hargreaves realised that if a number of spindles were placed upright and side by side, several threads might be spun at once. This gave the means of spinning twenty or thirty threads at once, with no more effort than had been previously required to spin a single thread. He called this the Spinning Jenny and, although it was initially welcomed by the hand spinners, when the price of yarn fell the mood changed. Fellow spinners marched on his cottage and destroyed his machines. In 1767, the year after Jedediah Strutt's patent, he fled to Nottingham where he worked as a carpenter. With Thomas James as a partner, they establishing a small cotton mill in a little street off Wollaton Street and the Hargreaves family lived in an adjacent house. The mill gave the street the name Mill Street, but it was afterwards changed to Bow Street. On 12 June 1770, James Hargreaves was granted a patent for the Spinning Jenny but he died eight years later.

James Hargreaves had patented a hand-operated machine responsible for mechanising spinning. The cotton hosiery industry of Nottingham benefited from the increased provision of yarn, but the Spinning Jenny was confined to producing cotton weft. It was unable to produce yarn of sufficient strength and quality for the warp as the thread was prone to break. Others took up the challenge, and among them was a Lancashire barber called Richard Arkwright, whose fertile brain began working out how he could produce a high-quality warp and a means by which machinery could replace hand labour.

Richard Arkwright

Richard Arkright concentrated single-mindedly on his new invention. This was often in secret as everyone in the cotton trade was suspicious of a machine that might cause mass unemployment in the industry. Despite all the hours spent working on the machine, it was still far from being perfected and, by 1768, with funds running alarmingly low, he transported his spinning machine to Nottingham – already an established area for stocking making. Arkwright's single-minded determination eventually paid off and with the financial help of two wealthy stocking manufacturers – Samuel Need of Nottingham and Jedediah Strutt of Derby – who he'd met in the Nottingham bank of Ichabod Wright, Arkwright built his cotton mill (a roller-spinning machine capable of being linked to an external source of power). The machinery was powered by a horse walking round a gin circle, but this needed space. The horse also needed feeding, tending and rest, so the next challenge was to find an improved source of power.

For this, Arkwright moved on to the water frame, which was the name given to the spinning frame when waterpower is used to drive it. This wasn't new; the ground had been prepared for him by such eminent engineers as Sorocold, who had perfected the first water-powered English silk mill in Derby in the early years of the eighteenth century. Fifty years later, Arkwright refined the process. He used the power of a waterwheel to drive a number of water frames, assembled with hundreds of spinning heads that could be operated by an unskilled worker. Each head effectively replaced a human spinner, drastically reducing the amount of labour needed and the time required to produce thread. To operate this, he needed to harness the energy and intensity of a reliable, constant and controllable source of water, and this he found at Cromford on the River Derwent in Derbyshire. Arkwright developed the idea and perfected the technique to spin raw cotton into thread using the first water-powered spinning frames. Richard Arkwright had put in place the system of production that earned him the title of 'father of the factory system'.

Samuel Crompton

Building on the work of James Hargreave and Richard Arkwright, who had both lived and worked in Nottingham, Samuel Crompton invented the spinning mule. As a boy Samuel had to contribute to the family resources by spinning yarn on James Hargreaves' Spinning Jenny. He saw its deficiencies and decided to improve it. For five or six years he worked in secret, the effort absorbing all his spare time and money. Around 1779, he succeeded in producing a Mule-Jenny, which later became known as the Spinning Mule. There was a strong demand for the yarn that Crompton was making, but he lacked the means and knowledge to take out a patent. He was ill-advised to show his machine in public, expecting payment of £200. All he got was £60 and, as the mule was unpatented, others soon manufactured it.

In 1811, he toured the 650 working cotton mills within the 60-mile radius of Bolton, gathering evidence of how widely the Spinning Mule had been adopted. He found that of the spindles in use, 155,880 were on Hargreaves' Jenny, 310,516 were on Arwright's water-frame and 4,600,000 were on Crompton's Mule. Around 80 per cent of the cotton goods bleached in Lancashire were woven on mule-spun cotton, and 700,000 people were directly or indirectly dependent on mule-spun yarn for their livelihood. The Spinning Mule had become the mainstay of cotton spinning in Britain, yet Crompton was almost destitute.

He took his evidence to parliament in 1812 expecting £50,000 compensation, but timing was against him – the national economy was funding the Napoleonic Wars. He was awarded just £5,000. With the aid of this money, Crompton started a business as a bleacher and then as a cotton merchant and spinner, but without success. He was dogged by bad luck and died with debts that exceeded his paltry assets, valued at only £25.

Lace

Lacemaking is an ancient craft created when a thread is looped, twisted or braided to other threads independently from a backing fabric. Objects resembling lace bobbins have been found in Roman remains, but there are no records of Roman lacemaking. The word lace (*las* in old English) means 'noose' or 'loop'.

In the fifteenth and early sixteenth century, lace was handmade using linen, silk, gold, or silver threads. It was dominant in both fashion and home décor. In the late sixteenth century, there was a rapid development in the field of lace for enhancing the beauty of collars and cuffs. Lace was used by clergy of the early Catholic Church as part of vestments in religious ceremonies. The popularity of lace increased rapidly and the cottage industry of lace making spread throughout Europe.

Moving on from the invention of the stocking frame, many ingenious mechanics tried unsuccessfully to modify this to manufacture point-net lace in which the mesh was looped in the same way as handmade lace. It needed to look delicate but be durable, and in trying to achieve this, the finished work was weak and frail. Samuel Cartledge of Nottingham is credited with the invention of a strong cotton thread suitable for the manufacture of British lace, but for many years no one discovered how the knitting frame could be adapted to twist the mesh of threads round each other.

Many tried and failed. These men, too numerous to mention, were using various modifications on the stocking frame. To knit stockings, just one thread is used in a uniform way, but to knit lace many threads are required to create a pattern. Ordinary weaving differs from lace weaving because it has the warp perpendicular instead of horizontal. Instead of the shuttle moving at right angles, brass bobbins in brass carriages of a very curious and delicate structure were made to pass in cross directions round the warp thread obliquely to produce the hexagonal meshes.

A guy named Hammond was probably the first to make a net from the stocking frame, but that is not quite certain as competition was fierce. Many had such limited finances they couldn't afford the cost of a patent, which varied from £100–£700. Additional expenses could be incurred if the inventor was forced to defend his patent at common law sometimes against a spurious contender. Lacking the necessary funds, mechanics were often prevented from reaping the fruits of their ingenuity. A Nottingham journeyman stocking maker named Flint conceived the idea of a point-net machine. Although this greatly benefited the town, he died in St Mary's poorhouse. As always, entrepreneurs were eager to secure patent rights on inventions that promised to yield a high rate of return. James Fisher, an influential lace merchant operating in London and Nottingham, was one such merchant.

The next step was the invention of the warp frame around 1775. There were five claimants for this, but the invention is believed to have belonged to a Londoner named Crane. William Herbert was the son of a framework knitter and worked in the stocking trade. He adapted a warp frame and produced tatting, cords and braiding. In 1791, a guy named Dawson worked on a number of these machines in Turncalf Alley later Sussex Street, Nottingham. He patented a machine that made plait stay-laces and military sashes, but when the patent expired and was not renewed, his livelihood was taken away and he committed suicide.

Richard Birkin was born at Belper in 1805, the son of a calico weaver. In 1822, he moved to New Basford where he learned to work a bobbin-net machine and produce a pearl edge on lace. He also perfected the technique for producing spots and honeycombs without stoppages. He was the juror for lace at the Great Exhibition in 1851 and was three times Mayor of Nottingham. His many improvements were continued by his son, Sir Thomas I. Birkin.

John Heathcoat and the Bobbin-Net Machine

John Heathcoat was born in August 1783 in Duffield, Derbyshire. At the age of sixteen, while apprenticed to a frame-smith near Loughborough, he conceived the idea of a machine for making lace similar to Buckingham or French lace. Firstly, he made a practical improvement in the construction of the warp-frame and succeeded in producing mitts of a lace-like appearance. At twenty-one, he arrived in Nottingham determined to pursue the study of mechanical lacemaking. He obtained work as a frame-smith and setter-up of machines at a shop between Broad Street and Beck Lane, now Heathcoat Street, renamed after him. He received 25s a week, but soon this had increased to 3 guineas a week. Shortly after this, he purchased his master's business, married and lived in Long Stairs. Showing great ingenuity and perseverance, he first studied the art of making the Buckingham or pillow-lace by hand, then replicated the same motions by mechanical means. It was a long and laborious task, but he succeeded in making the bobbin-net machine. In 1808, he took out a patent for traversed bobbin-net, formed by crossing and twisting the threads.

Meddling, invasive competitors infringing his privacy forced Heathcoat to leave Nottingham and move to Hathern, near Loughborough in Leicestershire, where he went into partnership with Charles Lacy, a Nottingham manufacturer. There, in 1808, he constructed a machine capable of producing an exact imitation of real pillow-lace. This machine-made lace was called English net or bobbin net and he patented his invention in 1809. At that time, it was by far the most expensive and complex textile apparatus in existence. In 1836, when describing the process of his invention, Heathcoat said: 'The single difficulty of getting the diagonal threads to twist in the

John Heathcoat's bobbin-net
machine, 1809.

allotted space was so great that, if now to be done, I should probably not attempt its
accomplishment.'

In 1816, their factory was attacked by Luddites and thirty-nine lace frames were
destroyed causing £10,000 worth of damage. Ten of the men were apprehended for the
felony, and eight of them were executed. John Heathcoat made a successful claim upon
the county for compensation, but when the magistrate stipulated that the money was
to be spent in the county of Leicester, he refused and moved the business to Tiverton
in Devon where it became very successful and established the Tiverton lacemaking
industry.

John Heathcoat's invention gave Nottingham a trade, which within fifty years
quadrupled its population and gave employment to probably 150,000 workpeople.

John Leavers

Some important improvements were made in 1813 by John Leavers, a frame-smith
and setter-up who moved to Nottingham from Sutton-in-Ashfield. He carried on his
operations for the construction of point net and warp lace machinery in a garret in
St Helen's Street near Canning Circus on the northern side of Derby Road. When
John Leavers needed carriages and bobbins of sufficient thinness for the necessary
improvements, they were made for him by Benjamin Thompson, the father of Bendigo,
England's champion prize-fighter (*see Famous Nottingham Characters*). For two years,
John Leavers practically isolated himself, and when his machine was complete his

John Leaver's lace making machine,
1828–46.

invention helped to lay the foundation of the machine lace trade in England. A modern version of the Leaver's machine is used to this day to produce the finest lace in the world. Some of the original nineteenth-century lace machines are still in use today, often interfaced with computers.

Gassing the Lace

Alongside the improvements and patents taken out by so many people, the family of Robert Hall of Basford needs a special mention. Robert Hall was a scientist who was one of the very first to use chloride of lime in bleaching. His son, Marshall Hall, entered the medical profession and was trained at the Nottingham General Hospital, but his second son Samuel went into the lace business.

A defect of cotton thread in comparison to linen is its fuzziness, which blurred the pattern detail of the lace, but, in 1817, Samuel Hall discovered a way to remove the fuzziness and loose fibres by singeing them away. The process known as gassing involved passing the thread net or lace through flames of hydrogen drawn up to a height of about ½ inch by a vacuum above so that the flame surrounded the material to be cleared without any injury to the fabric. The process was improved and patented in 1823 to give a previously unknown sharpness, clarity and transparency to the lace. In several magazines, Samuel Hall advertised his gassed thread under the name Urling. He charged ¾*d* a square yard and gassed around 5,000,000 square yards a year; Samuel Hall became a very rich man.

13

CRIME AND PUNISHMENT

The 1811 Depression and the 1812 Luddite Riots

The name Luddite is said to derive from a hand weaver called Ned Lud. When told by his employer to work harder, he reputedly picked up a hammer and demolished his weaving frame. His example was followed by others who took his name. That's the romantic view. The truth is more gritty.

In 1811, there was a great depression in the hosiery trade and many workmen had no means of subsistence. Excessive rent was charged for frames let out to workmen to use in their own homes, but with no work, these burdensome frames stood idle. On 11 March, there was a meeting of the framework knitters from the villages, when many threats of vengeance were made against some of the manufacturers who had reduced the prices they paid their workers for making stockings. The military appeared and the crowd was broken up, but that night, sixty-three frames were broken at Arnold. In the early months of 1811, the first threatening letters from Gen. Ned Ludd and the Army of Redressers were sent to employers in Nottingham. When this had no effect, during the next few weeks 200 more machines were broken. Gen. Ned Ludd and the Army of Redressers became known as Luddites and began to break into factories at night on a regular basis. In March 1811, several attacks were taking place every night. The Nottingham authorities had to enrol 400 special constables to protect the factories. Between 1811–16, 1,000 stocking frames and a large number of lace machines were destroyed in Nottinghamshire, and many more in the neighbouring counties of Derbyshire, Yorkshire, Lancashire and Leicestershire. The mills were armed against possible Luddite attack and the authorities enrolled special constables to protect the factories.

The distress was such that in Nottingham, on 30 January 1812, 4,248 families consisting of 15,340 individuals (nearly half the population) were relieved out of the poor rates. In 1817, the *Nottingham Review* reports an appeal from the framework knitters at Hoveringham, which stated that their average earnings were only 9s per week. After deductions had been made for frame rent, house rent, coal and candles, etc. only 2s remained.

These Luddite outrages continued from 1811 to 1816. London police, magistrates and officers were sent to assist in discovering the ringleaders and a secret committee was formed. Large funds were also provided. A Royal Proclamation was issued offering

Luddites smashed the frames.

a £50 reward for 'giving information on any person or persons wickedly breaking the frames', but to no avail. In February 1812, the government of Spencer Perceval proposed that machine-breaking should become a capital offence.

Lord Byron, living at nearby Newstead abbey, saw the problems first hand. In his Maiden Speech in the House of Lords on 27 February 1812, while forcibly describing the terrible state of affairs, opposed the death penalty. He said:

> During the short time I recently passed in Nottingham, not twelve hours elapsed without some fresh act of violence; and on that day I left the county I was informed that forty Frames had been broken the preceding evening, as usual, without resistance and without detection.
>
> Such was the state of that county, and such I have reason to believe it to be at this moment. But whilst these outrages must be admitted to exist to an alarming extent, it cannot be denied that they have arisen from circumstances of the most unparalleled distress: the perseverance of these miserable men in their proceedings, tends to prove that nothing but absolute want could have driven a large, and once honest and industrious, body of the people, into the commission of excesses so hazardous to themselves, their families, and the community.
>
> They were not ashamed to beg, but there was none to relieve them: their own means of subsistence were cut off, all other employment preoccupied; and their excesses, however to be deplored and condemned, can hardly be subject to surprise.
>
> As the sword is the worst argument than can be used, so should it be the last. In this instance it has been the first; but providentially as yet only in the scabbard. The present measure will, indeed, pluck it from the sheath; yet had proper meetings been

held in the earlier stages of these riots, had the grievances of these men and their masters [for they also had their grievances] been fairly weighed and justly examined, I do think that means might have been devised to restore these workmen to their avocations, and tranquillity to the country.

Despite this passionate speech by Lord Byron in the House of Lords, that same year Parliament passed the Frame Breaking Act, whereby people convicted of machine-breaking were sentenced to death. The Act continued in force for two years. As a further precaution, the government ordered 12,000 troops into the areas where the Luddites were active.

Byron became a strong advocate of social reform and was one of the few men in parliament to defend the actions of the Luddites. His political views also influenced the subject matter of his poems, an important example of this being the 'Song of the Luddites' written on 24 December 1816:

> As the Liberty lads o'er the sea
> Brought their freedom, and cheaply with blood,
> So we, boys, we
> Will die fighting, or live free,
> And down with all kings by King Ludd!
> When the web that we weave is complete,
> And the shuttle exchanged for the sword,
> We will fling the winding sheet
> O'er the despot at our feet,
> And dye it deep in the gore he has pour'd.
> Though black as his heart its hue,
> Since his veins are corrupted to mud,
> Yet this is the dew
> Which the tree shall renew
> Of Liberty, planted by Ludd!

The Pentrich Revolution of 1817

Matters were not helped when the Napoleonic Wars came to an end in 1815. Thousands of men were released from the forces, but, unable to find work, discontentment grew as many families were reduced to living in poverty. The workhouses were filled to capacity and all over the country seditious societies sprang up.

Jeremiah Brandreth was born in 1790 in Wilford – a village close to the centre of the city of Nottingham. Brandreth moved to Sutton-in-Ashfield where he found work as a stocking maker, but the industry was in trouble. It is believed that Brandreth was involved in Luddite activities in 1811. Six years later, aged twenty-seven and out of work and with a wife and three children to support, Jeremiah Brandreth decided to do something about it. In May 1817, he organized a meeting at the White Horse Inn in Pentrich where many had relied upon the struggling hosiery industry. He outlined his plans to march to London and overthrow Lord Liverpool's unpopular government, but among the crowd was William J. Oliver, a spy working for the government. It is widely believed that Brandreth was a victim of the then Home Secretary, Lord Sidmouth, who took severe measures against Luddite rioters.

Brandreth was known as the Nottingham Captain, and the first part of Brandreth's plan was that he and his fellow conspirators were to lead a march on Nottingham where they would receive 100 guineas, bread, meat and ale. They would then lead an attack on the local barracks. Ultimately, they would overthrow the government and end poverty forever. Because of Brandreth's strong personality and commanding presence, coupled with his promise of a better life after their victory, very few hesitated. On 9 June 1817, around 400 men and boys set off.

Arriving at Langley Mill, they heard that soldiers from Nottingham were on their way. Panic set in, and the men, ignoring Brandeth's threats, began to quickly disperse. Many escaped but around forty were arrested and sent to Derby gaol.

Trials for treason began on 15 October and lasted for ten days. Thirty-five people were brought to trial. Most of the insurrectionists were pardoned and Weightman was transported. The other three ringleaders – Jeremiah Brandreth, Isaac Ludlam and William Turner – were sentenced to be hanged, drawn and quartered, but the sentence of quartering was commuted by the Prince Regent. The three conspirators were the last people to be beheaded with an axe in Britain when executions took place at Derby on 7 November 1817.

Nottingham Barracks

When it was necessary to call in the troops, they were quartered in a very indiscriminate manner and townspeople were compelled to accommodate men-at-arms, whether they desired their company or not. Later, the difficulties and inconveniences of this system were recognised, so soldiers were billeted on various innkeepers. At first the innkeepers were glad to have them and the revenue they brought with them, but as discipline was sadly lacking the Nottingham innkeepers soon got tired of their somewhat unruly guests and the whole system of billeting fell into disrepute.

In 1792, it was decided to build a cavalry barracks on the summit of Nottingham Park on land given by the Duke of Newcastle. The foundation of the barracks was laid on the 6 August 1792. The buildings were of brick and contained quarters for the men and officers and a hospital. The whole was surrounded by an extensive yard enclosed within a brick wall. The presence of the cavalry in Nottingham was rendered all the more necessary in the early days of the nineteenth century by considerable industrial troubles.

The barracks were used as the cavalry headquarters of the East Midland District until 1855, when they were moved to Sheffield. It was out of these barracks that the Scots Greys marched on their departure to the campaign of Waterloo and again upon their departure for the Crimea on 3 July 1854. Very scanty remains of the barracks are left nowadays except the name Barrack Lane, off Derby Road.

The Reform Bill

For many years prior to 1831, people had criticised the electoral system as unfair. Only 5 per cent of the population in England and Wales had the right to vote, depending upon a person's wealth. If you were male, a 40s freeholder, a small landowner or wealthier, you were entitled. There were constituencies known as 'rotten boroughs', with only a handful of voters that elected two members of parliament. With no secret ballot, it was easy for candidates to buy votes, yet the new industrial towns that had grown during the previous eighty years had no MP to represent them.

On 10 October 1831, the House of Commons passed a Reform Bill, but the House of Lords, dominated by Tories, defeated it. Rioting followed with serious disturbances in London, Birmingham, Derby, Nottingham, Leicester, Yeovil, Sherborne, Exeter and Bristol. Rioters attacked the gaols and liberated the prisoners. People looted and burned down buildings including Nottingham Castle and Colwick Hall, home of Jack Musters, magistrate for Nottinghamshire, High Sheriff of Nottinghamshire in 1777, and Lt-Col. of the 1st regiment of the Nottingham Militia.

Colwick Hall

One of the finest buildings in Nottingham, Colwick Hall occupies a site that has been inhabited since Saxon days. Standing as it does on the northern bank of the River Trent, it's recorded in the Domesday Book as having a watermill. There are still traces of an artificial water course that conducted the river water to turn the mill that stood just below the hall. This caused a few disputes, because at one time so much water was taken that the navigation of the River Trent was impeded.

The first use of the name Colwick as a surname occurs when Reginald de Colwick witnessed a charter on 17 November 1225. A curious thing about Colwick is that rent appears to have been paid in weapons of war. In 1280, Sir Reginald de Colwick held his lands 'of the fee of Peveril by twelve barbed arrows'. In 1504, Colwick was held 'by the service of twelve crossbows yearly if asked for'.

On the death of William de Colwick in 1362, the estate passed by marriage into the Byron family who held it until around 1660, when it was purchased by Sir John Musters. All the older buildings disappeared when in 1775/76, the present hall was erected in the Palladian style to designs by the architect John Carr of York.

In 1805, Jack Musters (1777–1849), the eldest son of John Musters and his wife, Sophia, married Mary Ann Chaworth (1786–1832), heiress to the Chaworth estates in Annesley, Edwalton and Wiverton. Annesley was the neighbouring property to Newstead abbey, the Byron seat, and Mary Ann was the first love of George Gordon, the poet and 6th Lord Byron. They first met in 1803 when Byron was fifteen. He later wrote: 'Had I married Miss Chaworth, perhaps the whole tenor of my life would have been different.' She was the subject of his poems, including 'The Dream' and was described by him as the last of a time-honoured race.

The Musters were an established Nottinghamshire family, but in consequence of his marriage, Jack Musters took the surname Chaworth by Royal Licence and their eight children were given the name Chaworth. However, the family reverted to Musters in 1823. In 1827, Jack inherited Colwick Hall, but four years later tragedy struck.

On 10 October 1831, Colwick Hall was sacked by rioters from Nottingham, enraged at the failure of the Second Reform Bill. They attacked the house, armed amongst other things with the iron railings that they had torn from Notinton Place. After smashing and looting the contents they set fire to the building and watched it burn.

John Musters was away, but Mary Ann Musters, whose health was already poor, managed to escape with the help of her daughter Sophia. They hid in a shrubbery in the cold and rain overnight in fear of their lives. Mary Ann Musters was so traumatised by her ordeal that she never recovered from the shock. She died four months later on 6 February 1832 at Wiverton Hall.

Colwick Hall was restored, but after the death of Jack Musters in 1849 it was rarely used by members of the Chaworth-Musters family, who preferred Annesley or Wiverton. The contents were sold at auction in 1850 and the house let to tenants. It was sold by John P. Chaworth-Musters to the Nottingham Racehorse Co. in 1896, and after years of neglect Colwick Hall was restored and reopened as a country house hotel and conference centre in 2003.

When the rioters wrecked the hall in 1831, they appear to have thrown the decorative wrought iron gateways into the lake, where they lay rusting and forgotten for many years. These fine examples of Nottingham wrought-iron work, made around 1776 and contemporary to the hall, were later discovered and recovered. One now stands at the entrance to the nearby churchyard and the second gate is preserved in Nottingham Castle.

Gallows Hill

As its name implies, Gallows Hill was where the gallows were set up on one of the highest hills in Nottingham. It was a large area of open ground because hangings were well-attended public spectacles. In an era when trials and punishment were often the only form of entertainment available to the peasants, these occasions qualified as a half-day holiday. They were administered in a sort of carnival atmosphere. Trinkets and mementoes were sold, jugglers and clowns entertained while vendors sold fruit and snacks. Even for petty theft, punishable with a day in the stocks or pillory, the crowd amused themselves throwing rotten vegetables at the culprit.

It was obviously used for other forms of entertainment too, with or without the hanging. In the tales of Robin Hood, when Robin heard a crier proclaiming that the Sheriff of Nottingham was holding an archery competition (the prize being an arrow with a silver shaft and feathers of red gold), he disguised himself as a vagabond and took part. The archery tournament was held on the level piece of ground near Gallows Hill. Scaffolding seating was set up for the sheriff and his lady, the officers of the city and numerous knights. Nearby stood the marshals who would oversee the tournament and ensure that the rules were followed. The first challenge was to shoot at a broad target placed at 22 yards distance. After each round, the target was moved 10 yards further away until it was placed at 300 yards. The target was then removed and a wand set up in its place. The object was to strike the wand that was moved progressively further away. Having split the wand in two, Robin was declared the winner.

In days gone by, the miserable criminals had to wend their way from the county and town prisons up the Mansfield Road to meet their doom on Gallows Hill. Gradually, the custom arose that the landlord of the Nag's Head on Mansfield Road, which stood just at the point where the gallows came into view, should provide the unfortunates with a last drink of Nottingham ale. On one occasion a criminal was on his way to his execution and, arriving at the Nag's Head, instead of partaking of the customary refreshment, he put it on one side and went on to his death. Scarcely had life left his body when a messenger arrived bringing with him a reprieve, which was too late to prevent the death of the poor unfortunate man hanging on the gallows. If he had not rejected that last drink of Nottingham ale, he would have been saved. The last person to be hanged on Gallows Hill was William Wells, indicted for highway robbery on 2 April 1827.

The Galleries of Justice

When the Normans conquered the Saxons and decided to divide Nottingham into the French and English boroughs, each had its own laws, administered from separate sites. The English borough was in the area now known as the Lace Market, and on High Pavement is the site where the law had been administered for almost 1,000 years. It's now the Galleries of Justice, also known as the Shire Hall – an independently run museum.

The earliest confirmed use of the site for official purposes dates back to the eleventh century when the Normans were the masters who appointed sheriffs to keep the peace and collect taxes from the English. Hence the site was also referred to as the Sheriff's

The courtroom.

Hall, the County Hall or the King's Hall. There has been a court of justice here since 1375, the date of the first written record of the site being used as a law court with the courtrooms dating back to the fourteenth century and the gaol dating back to at least 1449 – the year the town was given county status and was cut off from the county. Henry VI purposely excluded the King's Hall/Shire Hall and ordered it to be left under the old jurisdiction because the hall had long been recognised as the gaol for the counties of Nottingham and Derby.

Over the centuries, the courts and prison have been developed and enlarged. The Hall was rebuilt between 1769–72 at a cost of £2,500. The architect was James Gandon of London and the builder was Joseph Pickford of Derby.

The present Georgian building has been in use since 1780, with additional wings added and changes made between 1820 and 1840. A grand jury room was added in 1859. The building was fronted by an iron palisade to help control unruly crowds on the occasion of a public hanging. The last was held in 1864 when Richard Thomas Parker, aged twenty-nine, was hanged for murdering his mother.

In 1876, the front was redesigned and major improvements made. Three stone cut-outs now cover the holes on the steps of the Shire Hall where the gallows were dropped in. Within a few weeks, a fire broke out and the courts needed to be largely rebuilt. In the meantime, the prison gaol closed in 1878 due to appalling conditions and lay empty between 1878 and 1995. A working police station opened in 1905. On this historic site, an individual could be arrested, sentenced and executed.

The courts and the police station closed in 1986, but the hall continued in use as Nottingham's civil and criminal courts until 1991, when Nottingham Crown Court was opened at Canal Street. The whole was then turned into a museum housed in the former courtroom, gaol and police station. Visitors can go down into the underground gaol and exercise yard where executions took place, experience what it was like on a convict ship and marvel at the special exhibitions.

The Suicide's Graveyard

Canning Circus is a busy junction where five major roads – Alfreton Road, Ilkeston Road, Derby Road and Wollaton Street – meet and cross. Thousands of people circumnavigate the roundabout daily, but few glance across at the striking building that forms the arched entrance to the general cemetery at this busy junction. Even less question why it's here at a junction of so many major roads. This land was not developed until the late eighteenth century. It had started life as a muddy area of interconnecting trackways outside the city wall, and the last resting place for those poor souls not allowed to be buried in consecrated ground. In olden days, crossroads were selected as a suitable place to bury suicides.

The point where roads intersect has long been associated with magic and evil. Hecate, the Greek goddess of witchcraft, was also goddess of crossroads and animals were sacrificed to her there. Witches were alleged to gather at crossroads in order to conjure up the devil and his demons, and practice black magic. Some spells were considered to be more effective if they were cast at a crossroads. The evil reputation of crossroads was enhanced by the fact that it was often the site of the local gallows.

A water carrier damping down the dust at the Cannning Circus; the suicides graveyard is seen on the left.

The bodies of undesirables were habitually buried at crossroads. It showed the persons marginal position in society or because no parish would acknowledge them. Some say it was to confuse the ghost of the deceased who would be unable to decide which road to get back home to stop them haunting. The interment was usually performed hastily and at night, without any form of religious ceremony. There are a considerable number of such burials noted in the records of Nottingham.

Burial customs and beliefs are very curious. For example, the wearing of black during the period of mourning is another strange survival from the past. The primitive belief was that after death the spirit still continued to linger and as long as the body was allowed to remain in its accustomed surroundings, the spirit was more or less content. But when the body was taken elsewhere for burial, the spirit became homesick and fretful and vented its spite upon the relatives who had taken it from its familiar surroundings. To escape this resentment, it was necessary for the relatives to disguise themselves by wearing mourning clothes in unaccustomed black. Gradually, the belief in the resentment of the spirit evaporated, but the custom of wearing black continued.

14

NOTTINGHAM'S MAJOR INDUSTRIES IN THE NINETEENTH AND TWENTIETH CENTURIES

In the nineteenth and twentieth century, the main industries in Nottingham were textiles, tobacco, bicycles, pharmaceuticals and printing. World renowned for machine lace, Nottingham also had the big players – Raleigh Bicycle Co., Boots the Chemist and Player's cigarettes.

The Lace Centre of England

Willoughby's Directory of 1799 lists the trades and occupation in Nottingham as 149 hosiers and 6 lacemakers. Around 1810, the hosiery industry ran into trouble because of a fall in demand due to changes in fashion when men preferred to wear trousers instead of stockings. The hosiery business was in deep depression, which lasted until the mid-nineteenth century, but in Nottingham the decline in demand for hosiery was offset by the rise in demand for lace. In 1832, the first edition of William White's *History, Gazetteer and Directory of Nottingham* shows that the hosiery trade had almost expired and there was a new industry – bobbin-net makers.

There were 257 bobbin-net makers in Nottingham and a further 546 bobbin-net makers in the villages around the town. Bobbin-net makers were lace-makers who employed a machine and sold their net in the brown state. The circumstances that had led to this remarkable and rapid rise of a new industry was known as the bobbin-net fever. It was the result of the expiration of John Heathcoat's patent for mechanically producing lace.

Anyone who had a little capital could buy a bobbin-net machine and make brown net on it in their own homes. The brown lace was not the finished article. It had to be gassed to remove imperfections, cut, mended, bleached, dyed and finished with embroidered loops and picots before it could be sold as lace for collars, dresses, edging for other garments and, increasingly, for lace curtains.

Lace finishing like this
establishment of K. Burrows
on Short Hill became a
necessary trade in the
lace market.

These industries had been carried out as cottage industries, but, in 1832, White's directory listed 186 lace manufacturers and 70 hosiery manufacturers. These were the merchants and finishers who organised these operations with an increasingly female and child labour force. The machine-wrought lace industry was firmly established during the so-called twist net fever. Work was plentiful and the population grew.

In 1843, the *Nottingham Journal* referred to two groups of warehouses – the older one in the Hounds Gate/Castle Gate area, the newer one in St Mary's Gate, now referred to as the seat of the Lace Market. The Lace Market was the heart of the world's lace industry, but it was never a market in the sense of having stalls where goods were sold. It's a historic quarter-mile square packed with factories and warehouse that were used for making, finishing, storing, displaying and selling the lace.

The increase in lace output and trade was to be a dominant part of Nottingham's economy in the second half of the nineteenth century. *White's Directory*, published in 1902, shows the dominance of the lace trade. There were 178 lacemakers, many of them in the thirty tenement factories that housed several different firms, which had been built in the last thirty years or so. By contrast, there were 249 lace manufacturers and over 200 of these were in the Lace Market or close by. The lace industry in the town of Nottingham employed over 20,000 people, the majority of them women. Their products were classed under three headings – lace for millinery, dresses and other ornamental uses, the curtain branch and the plain net branch.

In Kelly's 1932 directory for Nottinghamshire, the old distinction in earlier directories between lacemakers and lace manufacturers disappeared. The trade is divided into lace manufacturers and lace curtain manufacturers. The directory names 158 and 44 respectively, after allowing for a few firms that appeared in both. Of these 202 firms that covered the county of Nottinghamshire, 37 were outside the town mainly at Beeston and Chilwell and 120 were in or adjoining the Lace Market.

The outbreak of war in 1939 meant a disruption of normal trade, but the lace industry was adapted for wartime production, making such items as mosquito nets and camouflage netting. Although Nottingham did not experience the level of

A panel of Nottingham lace featuring the local hero, Robin Hood.

devastation from air raids that other towns did, by the end of the war the Lace Market was a rundown enclave; the tall warehouses blackened by decades of coal-burning in narrow streets with derelict and worn-out facilities. The diversification of uses and the unavailability of resources to maintain the buildings meant that they continued to deteriorate.

In common with the UK textile industry as a whole, Nottingham's textile sector fell into headlong decline in the decades following the Second World War as British manufacturers proved unable to compete on price or volume with output of factories in the Far East and South Asia. Very little textile manufacturing was taking place in Nottingham, but the city's heyday in this sector endowed it with some fine industrial buildings in the Lace Market district. By 1972, some thirty-five buildings or groups of buildings in the Lace Market had been listed, and in 1996 a review of the city's listed buildings increased this number to ninety-four. Nearly all of the old warehouses that were run down during the recession years have been cleaned, renovated and put to new use. The Lace Market area now has no connection with lace. These impressive examples of nineteenth-century industrial architecture have found new uses as luxury apartments, high-spec offices and academic buildings. Most of the area is typically Victorian, with densely packed four–seven-storey, red-brick buildings, iron railings, old gas lamps and red phone boxes, but High Pavement is a handsome Georgian street.

For the benefit of the many tourists that visit Nottingham castle, a Lace Centre was erected on Castle Road in 1970. Erected is an appropriate word to describe the building that was constructed here. This was fifteenth century merchant's house known as 'Severns' – a name that dates from 1735 when John and James Severn began a wine importing business on Middle Pavement. In 1956, the building was restored but it was not to remain much longer. In 1969, Middle Pavement was being revamped and Severn's, one of the oldest domestic properties in the city, was in danger of demolition. It was saved brick by brick and re-erected on Castle Road in 1970 to be opened as the Lace Centre.

A fifteenth-century merchant's
house – the oldest domestic
building in the city.

The Rayleigh Bicycle Co.

One of the oldest bicycle companies in the world was started in Nottingham in 1885
by Richard Morris Woodhead, from Sherwood Forest, and Paul Eugene Louis Angois.
They set up a small bicycle workshop in Raleigh Street, Nottingham, one of fifteen
bicycle manufacturers based in the town at that time. They chose Raleigh as their
brand name after the street, and their first advert appeared in the *Nottinghamshire
Guardian* on 15 May 1885.

   Two years later, William Ellis joined the partnership. Like Woodhead and Angois,
Ellis' background was in the lace industry. At this time, the Raleigh Bicycle Co. was
making about three cycles a week and employed around half a dozen men, but thanks
to Ellis' financial investment the bicycle works could expand. They moved round the
corner from Raleigh Street into former lace works on the adjoining Russell Street,
where the works comprised three small workshops and a greenhouse.

   In 1888, Frank Bowden replaced William Ellis as the partnership's principal investor.
He was allotted 5,000 £1 shares, while Woodhead and Angois between them held
another 5,000 shares.

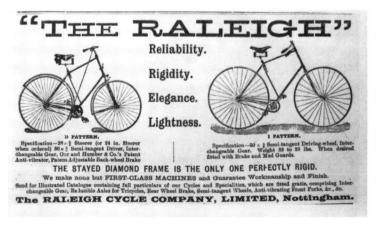

The Rayleigh advert,
*c.*1889.

To enable further expansion of the business, Bowden financed the renting of Clarke's five-storey former lace factory on Russell Street and the installation of new machinery. Raleigh expanded rapidly. By 1891, the company occupied not only Clarke's factory but also Woodroffe's Factory and Russell Street Mills. In November 1892, Raleigh signed a tenancy agreement for rooms in Butler's factory on the other side of Russell Street, and shortly after the company also occupied Forest Road Mill at the junction with Russell Street at the opposite end from Raleigh Street.

By 1913, Bowden had created a business that was claimed to be the biggest bicycle manufacturing company in the world, occupying 7½ acres in purpose-built premises, completed in 1897 at Faraday Road, Lenton, Nottingham. It subsequently became much bigger.

In 1899, Raleigh started to build motorcycles and in 1903, introduced the Raleighette – a belt-driven three-wheel motorcycle with the driver in the back and a wicker seat for the passenger between the two front wheels. Financial losses meant production only lasted until 1908.

In 1930, the company acquired the rights to the Ivy Karryall – a motorcycle fitted with a cabin for cargo and a hood for the driver. Raleigh's version was called the Light Delivery Van and had a chain drive. A two-passenger version was followed by Raleigh's first three-wheel car – the Safety Seven. It was a four-seat convertible with shaft drive and a maximum of 55 mph (89 km/h). A saloon version was planned, but Raleigh shut its motor department to concentrate on bicycles again. Chief designer T. L. Williams took the equipment and remaining parts and moved to Tamworth, where his company produced three-wheelers for sixty-five years. The leftover parts from Raleigh carried an 'R', so Williams chose a matching name – Reliant.

Raleigh also made mopeds in the late 1950s and '60s as the bicycle market declined. The most popular of which was the RM6 Runabout. This model featured unsprung front forks and a cycle type calliper front brake, which made it a very affordable mode of transport. Due to its success, production continued until February 1971, seventeen months after Raleigh had stopped manufacturing all other mopeds.

In 1958, Alan Sillitoe's debut novel, *Saturday Night and Sunday Morning*, is partly set in Raleigh's Nottingham factory where Sillitoe himself had been employed. Several scenes for the 1960 film adaptation starring Albert Finney were filmed on location at the factory.

During the war, bicycle production was down to 5 per cent as the factory produced fuses. For much of the post-war era, the British bicycle market was in decline with the increasing affordability and popularity of the automobile. Raleigh diversified into lightweight sports racer bicycles, considerably lighter and quicker than any previous models. In 1965, Raleigh introduced the RSW16, which had small wheels, an open frame and built-in luggage carrying capacity. Five years later, they introduced a children's bike they called the Raleigh Chopper. It proved to be an icon of the age and almost single-handedly rescued Raleigh, selling millions worldwide. The Raleigh Chopper remained in production until 1982, when the rising popularity of the BMX bicycle caused sales to drop off.

Production was now in England, America and Japan. By 1984, all Raleighs for the American market, except the top-of-the range Team Professional, made in Ilkeston, Nottingham, and Prestige road bikes made in Nottingham were produced in the Far

Rayleigh workshop where *Saturday Night and Sunday Morning* was filmed in 1960.

East. The high-end, one of a kind bicycles and framesets were produced in Ilkeston Special Bicycle Developments Unit (SBDU) from 1974 to 1989, then production was moved to a new Raleigh Special Products division in Nottingham.

In 1999, Raleigh ceased volume production of frames in the UK. By 2003, assembly of bicycles had also ended in the UK. The new millennium saw bicycles made in Vietnam and other centres of low-cost, high-quality production with the final assembly taking place in Germany.

Raleigh's long association with cycle sport continues. The company's special products division make race frames, including those used by the Raleigh professional team of the 1970s. During the 1980s, Raleigh also supported British professional teams and sponsored a mountain bike team in the early 1990s that also raced in road events. In 2009, it was announced that the company would be creating a new cycling team called Team Raleigh that has gone on to many high-profile wins.

Boots the Chemist
John Boot was born in 1815 in Radcliffe of Trent, Nottinghamshire, to a farming family, but illness forced him to give up farm work and look for a change of career to support his wife Mary and two young children, Jesse and Jane. That's how he started making and selling herbal remedies. He was not trained as a chemist, but, using the herbal remedies his mother made, he learned his profession as he experimented. In 1849, at the age of thirty-four, John Boot opened his herbalist shop at No. 38 Goose Gate, Nottingham, but even as a chemist John Boot's health did not improve and he died in 1863.

His wife Mary carried on with the business as M & J Boot Herbalists, helped behind the counter by thirteen-year-old Jesse, born 2 June 1850. Jesse learnt through experience and gradually took over the responsibility of running the shop. Jesse Boot is listed in Kelly's directory for 1876 as a herbalist. The principle he adopted was 'large sales and small profits'. He put a notice in the shop window, as shown here in our photograph, stating that drugs and proprietary articles were for sale at reduced prices.

Although this was not popular with his fellow tradesmen, it certainly brought customers flocking to the little shop. His competitors spread the news that a man who could sell so cheaply could not sell the best and his goods could not be pure. It was partly in answer to this unfair criticism that Jesse Boot coined the phrase the 'Pure Drug Company'. He was running the business on the minimum of capital, and for this reason, he could not allow his customers credit, which is why it became known as Boots the Cash Chemist.

John Boot's first shop at Goose Gate, Nottingham.

In 1882, he leased Nos 16–20 Goose Gate for 100 years and then began rebuilding the premises to become a fully equipped chemist's shop. He opened more shops in Lincoln and Sheffield. In the 1880s and still in his early thirties, Jesse Boot suffered a breakdown in health and went to the Channel Islands to recuperate. It was there that he met his future wife, Florence Rowe, the daughter of a Jersey bookseller.

In 1883, there was a change of name to Boot & Co. Ltd, then Boots Pure Drug Co. Ltd. in 1888. By 1896 there were sixty shops. In 1898, Jesse Boot began leasing space in what had previously been Hine and Mundella's steam-powered hosiery factory on Station Street, built in 1851. In 1912, he completed the purchase of the whole building for £22,000. As Jesse Boot extended his business, he acquired more buildings in the area until he owned almost all the property between the Midland Railway station and

Boots deliveries were made by horse and cart, 1903.

A napier van, one of Boot's extensive range of vehicles in the early 1920s.

the Nottingham canal. Now he had factories where he could produce the vast range of pharmaceutical and other goods manufactured under the Boot's name. In the First World War, Boots manufacture a wide range of goods for the troops. Boots were also responsible for the bulk of saccharin production in the country. This had previously been imported from the continent.

Boots majestic High Street store, built in 1903, was the model for many other Boots' department stores. As well as selling a great range of goods, the shop had a café and booklover's library. This shop closed in 1972 when Boots opened their branch in the Victoria Centre.

Jesse Boot was knighted in 1909 and created a baronet in 1917. In 1920, when Jesse Boot retired to the south of France and sold the company to the American United Drug Co. there were more than 600 shops.

In the New Year's Honours list of 1929, Jesse Boot was elevated to the peerage, and created Baron Trent of Nottingham in the County of Nottingham on 18 March 1929. Jesse Boot, 1st Baron Trent, had transformed Boots the Chemist founded by his father John into a national retailer, which branded itself 'Chemists to the Nation'.

Jesse Boot was a great benefactor to the City of Nottingham and was presented with the Freedom of the City in 1920. In the 1920s, Jesse Boot bought a large estate at Highfields with the idea of building a model factory on the land. Instead, he donated the land and gave £500,000 for the building of the university college there. It was opened in 1928 by King George V. The Sir Jesse Boot Chair in Chemistry at the university was named in his honour. Jesse Boot had a dream to build model factories providing ideal working conditions, surrounded by houses like those at Bournville and Port Sunlight. To do this, he bought a site at Beeston, but he died before the completion of his vision.

Jesse Boot died on 13 June 1931 in Villa Millbrook – his home in Jersey. Opposite the house stands St Matthew's church, at that time architecturally uninspiring and financially self-supporting, serving the community of Millbrook. Jesse had formed a friendship with René Lalique, the French glass artist, and Jesse's widow Florence asked if he would refurbish the interior of the church as a tribute to her husband. He readily agreed, creating a masterpiece in glass. It was dedicated in September 1934 when Lalique was seventy-four years old. Popularly known as the Glass church, this magnificent memorial to Jesse Boot is also a monument to the work of Rene Lalique, preserved in their memory.

Jesse's son John inherited the title of Baron Trent, and when Boots was sold back into British hands in 1933 he headed the company, but died without an heir in March 1956. Boots diversified into the research and manufacturing of drugs with its development of the ibuprofen painkiller during the 1960s. The company was awarded the Queen's Award for Technical Achievement for this in 1987. In 1968, Boots acquired the 622-strong Timothy Whites and Taylors Ltd. chain.

Boots expanded into Canada in 1978 by purchasing the Tamblyn Drugs chain. In 1982, the company opened a new manufacturing plant in Cramlington, Northumberland. In the early 1990s, Boots began to diversify and bought Do-It-All home furnishings chain and Halfords, the bicycle and car parts business. These were later sold. Boots Opticians Ltd was formed in 1987, and Boots diversified into dentistry in 1998 with a number of stores offering this service. It also made a venture into 'wellbeing' services, offering customers treatments ranging from facials, homeopathy and nutritional advice to laser-eye surgery and Botox. These services were abandoned in 2003. A subsequent merger with Alliance Unichem resulted in the name change to Alliance Boots and there are more sales and mergers taking place. There are outlets of Boots in most High Streets throughout the country 165 years after John Boot started that first shop.

The head office is still situated on the Boots Estate, located near the Nottingham suburb of Beeston, chosen by Jesse Boot in the 1920s. More buildings, including the two principal factory buildings and the former fire station, are Grade II listed. Set in landscaped grounds, the Millennium Garden features a herb garden with plants that Jesse used in his original herbal remedies. It's in the shape of a goose foot as a reminder of John Boot's original shop on Goose Gate in Nottingham.

Player's Cigarettes

Smoking is a very old habit that became fashionable as a cure for ulcers, headaches, asthma, indigestion, sore throats and even plague in the fifteenth century. It was popularized in England by Sir Walter Raleigh and even Queen Elizabeth was known to smoke a pipe. For centuries the pipe, mostly made of clay, was the most popular method of smoking.

John Player came to Nottingham from Saffron Walden in 1859 looking for work in the textile industry, as did a lot of other people at that time. He was twenty years old and obtained a job as a draper, but by 1861 he was established on his own as an agent for Prentice & Co., agricultural manures and seeds. He took a shop at No. 5 Beastmarket Hill, Nottingham, next to the cattle market and married and lived above the shop. He obliged his customers by keeping a tin or two of tobacco handy to sell in 'screws' costing a few pence each. Soon the sale of tobacco was proving more lucrative than the sale of seeds and fertiliser.

In 1868 John Player abandoned his agricultural manures and seeds to enter the tobacco trade and by 1871 he was registered as a tobacconist, producing packed tobacco under his own name. Virtually all tobacco at that time was sold loose so it was quite an innovation. Smokers would buy tobacco by weight and, if it wasn't smoked in a pipe, they'd buy cigarette papers to roll their own cigarettes. In 1874, John Player opened another shop in Market Street. By 1877, he was so successful that he bought a small tobacco factory at No. 45 Broadmarsh, previously owned and run by the tobacconist William Wright. His shops continued to do good trade and in 1878 he purchased a third shop at No. 5 Broad Street. By 1881, he was employing eighty people, a figure that grew as demand increased. In the local directory of 1884/85, John Player is registered as a tobacco cutter. He purchased land in Radford just west of the city centre so that another three factory blocks could be built. This became known as the Castle Works or Castle Tobacco Factory, a name that was emphasised by the registered trademark of the company – the image of Nottingham Castle.

The first block of the Castle Factory, alternatively known as No. 1 Factory, was opened in 1884 on Radford Boulevard and used to process and pack tobacco. The other two blocks were hired by lace manufacturers until Player's Co. grew enough to require the

John Player's original
factory, Broadmarsh.

extra space. At this time, No. 1 was one of the largest factories in the world, with one room
300 feet long by 60 feet wide; the machinery was driven by a 300-HP engine.
On 9 December 1884, John Player died, just months after the completion of the Castle
Factory on Radford Boulevard. A group of trusted associates ran the business until his two
sons, John Dane (1864–1949) and William Goodacre (1866–1959), were ready to take over.

Player's Navy Cut, the first branded cigarette, was marketed in 1879. In 1888, they
were selling in packets of twelve and it was claimed that sales exceeded 74,000 packets
a year, although this number may have included Castle Brand too. Demand for these
cigarettes was so high that the workforce had to be increased to approximately 500
employees and the remaining two factory blocks were needed.

Because early cigarettes were sold in paper packets, the contents were likely to get
crushed when carried in the pocket. To safeguard the contents, plain pieces of card
were inserted to stiffen the packet. Advertisements began to appear on these stiffeners
in 1878, and soon pictorial cards issued in sets on many subjects proved greatly
popular. The cigarette card was born.

The firm became a limited company in 1895 and John Dane Player and William
Goodacre Player became managing directors. By 1898, the workforce totalled 1,000.
Female employees, numbering 200, known as the 'Player's Angels', handmade up to
2,000 cigarettes per person per day.

John Dane and William Goodacre developed the company further and were one
of the biggest employers in the East Midlands. They were both made Freemen of the
City of Nottingham in 1934 in recognition of their benefactions and exceptional
contributions to the welfare of the local community.

In 1901, American millionaire James Buchanan Duke, head of the American Tobacco
Co., wanted to take over the business. To counteract this, within four months, Player's
united with Wills, Churchman's and many other tobacco firms to form the Imperial

Player's workers outside the main factory, Beckham Road, 1887.

Tobacco Co., John Dane and William Goodacre remained on the Imperial Board until their retirement in 1926.

Between 1910 and 1914, considerable expansions were made to the company. In 1910, the Imperial Board authorised the first bonus payment to all employees at the Castle Factory. Employment in the factories steadily increased until there were 2,500 people working in the factory by 1914. Trade increased after the outbreak of the war, and at Christmas 1914 every member of the forces received a presentation box of cigarettes and tobacco from Princess Mary.

In the 1920s, there was a change in the consumer profile. It became more acceptable for women to smoke and the act was seen as a symbol of sophistication, independence, upper-class rebellion, modernity and maturity. A major influence for smoking on young men and women were Hollywood films. As the cinema became more popular, more people saw iconic stars smoking cigars and cigarettes, so the consumer profile changed as the media industry evolved and demand increased.

By 1928, Player's had 5,000 employees and the advertising department was producing an average of 15,000 displays, stands and show-cards per week. To accommodate the extra workers, a new factory and the Bonded Warehouse on Triumph Road, which had the capacity of 20,000 tons of tobacco leaf, were built in 1932, opposite the Castle Factory on Radford Boulevard.

Two-thirds of all the cigarettes sold in Britain were Player's. In January 1937, Player's sold nearly 3.5 million cigarettes. By 1939, the workforce increased again to 7,500 employees. Unlike many factories, Player's was not affected by the Second World War. Demand was still extraordinarily high, but Player's had to change their form of packaging to material that was a lot thinner than the usual board until rationing ended in 1955.

In 1962, there was a report released by the Royal College of Physicians on Smoking and Health that detailed the dangers of smoking. Player's did not introduce health warnings on cigarette packets until 1971. A new factory named the Horizon Factory was opened in the early 1970s on Nottingham's industrial outskirts, with better road access and more effective floor space. The old factories in Radford, especially the cavernous No. 1 Factory, which occupied the whole area between Radford Boulevard and Alfreton Road, bordered by Player Street and Beckenham Road, were gradually

Player's head office *c.* 1950.

run down. The No. 2 Factory, facing onto Radford Boulevard with its distinctive clock now plinthed in the retail park on the site, and the No. 3 factory with its rooftop 'John Player & Sons' sign, were demolished in the late 1980s. On 15 April 2014, Imperial Tobacco announced that the Horizon Factory would close in early 2016, bringing an end to cigarette and tobacco manufacture in Nottingham after over 130 years.

A Saucy Story

In the late 1890s, a small time grocer named Frederick Gibson Garton was experimenting with sauces and chutneys in a room behind his shop at No. 47 Sandon Street, Basford. He developed a sauce that fulfilled Mrs Beeton's dictum that 'a sauce should not be too piquant on the one hand, or too mawkish on the other'. In his 1894 *The Grocers Diary*, Garton wrote down a recipe that included garlic, shallots, ground mace, tomato puree, cayenne pepper, ground ginger, raisons, flour, salt and vinegar. It sold well, and when he heard that a restaurant at the Houses of Parliament had begun serving it in 1895, he registered the name HP Sauce. But Frederick Garton had overstretched himself and owed money to the Midland Vinegar Co. One day, Edwin Samson Moore of the Midlands Vinegar Co. arrived in the shop to collect the unpaid debts. To get himself away from curious customers, Moore was ushered to the rear of the building where in a washhouse cooper, a sauce that smelt uncommonly good, was brewing.

Moore agreed to wipe out Garton's debts and give him £150 if he gave him the recipe and refrained from carrying on any trade connected with sauces and chutney in the future. Under duress, Garton agreed. On 25 May 1899, he signed an agreement transferring his business and giving Moore the recipes for HP Sauce, Daddies Favourite, Nottingham Relish, Sandon Sauce, Banquet Sauce, Yorkshire Sauce and Barton Co.'s Indian Chutney. Also, as part of the agreement, Garton had to go over to the factory in Birmingham show them how to make the sauce. His expenses were limited to £1 per day.

The Midland Vinegar Co., the forerunner of HP Foods, subsequently launched HP Sauce in 1903. It has been the best-selling brand of brown sauce in the UK for over 100 years, and in 2005 had 73.8 per cent of the retail market. One of the original bottles that has Garton's name embossed on the side is in possession of the Nottingham Castle Museums and Galleries.

15

TRANSPORT

River Trent

The River Trent, which can boast to be the third largest river in England, has its source in Staffordshire and flows through the Midlands forming a once significant boundary between the North and South of England. It's unusual among English rivers in that it flows north for the second half of its route to the Humber Estuary which empties into the North Sea between Hull and Immingham.

In 1110, it apparently dried up in places and the river has a history of freezing over due to its shallow water. During the great frost that lasted several weeks, in 1895, the River Trent froze over in Nottingham and crowds skated on it. Carts were driven across and fires were lit on the ice. The frost was so severe that it penetrated the ground so deeply that the water in the service mains was frozen.

The winter of 1946/47 saw extreme weather conditions similar to 1895. Freezing temperatures in January and February were followed by heavy rainfall in March. This, and the sudden thaw, caused widespread flooding equal to those first recorded in 1875. Flooding has been common throughout its history, and the name Trent is believed to be Celtic, meaning 'strongly flooding'.

The River Trent overflowed its banks and flooded one eighth of the city in 1946/47. The worst affected area was the low-lying Meadows. After these floods, the Trent River Board decided to take action and a flood defence scheme was undertaken. The River Leen overflowed its banks causing serious flooding in the surrounding streets and houses. The low-lying Boots site at Beeston was flooded and workers were transported by lorry through the floods, while trains ran through the floodwater at Basford Crossing.

The Trent Navigation Co., which existed from 1783 to 1940, was responsible for controlling and improving navigation on the river. By the Trent Navigation Transfer Act of 1915, the river was put under the control of Nottingham Corporation who implemented improvements which, when completed in 1927, enabled larger river boats to sail up to Nottingham from Hull and the continent. The width at the river at Trent Bridge is 290 feet.

Trent Bridge

It's possible that the Romans were the first to build a bridge over the River Trent. The Saxons did in AD 922 and Edward II did in 1156. The upkeep of the bridge was

A view of the old Trent Bridge.

considered a religious duty in the Middle Ages, and this bridge, which became known as the Heth Beth Bridge or old Trent Bridge, had a bridge chapel on it dedicated to St Mary. In 1202, the repairs and upkeep were undertaken by the brethren of the hospital of St John the Baptist, but this proved too much for them and the Archbishop of York had to make a general appeal. On 21 February 1551, the responsibility for repairing the bridge passed to Nottingham Corporation through a Royal Charter which created the Bridge Estate.

Disaster came to the bridge in 1334/35 when it was damaged by floods. No doubt it was built and repaired at different periods, then in the great frost that continued from September to March 1682/83 the ice tore away the northern half of the twelfth-century bridge. The repaired bridge had fifteen arches across the river, plus those over the floodplain. A Dr Thoroton wrote in 1677 that there was an arch of the bridge that was still known as Chapel Arch because that's where the bridge chapel had stood. Several fragments of stone windows and other parts of the chapel were dredged from the river under the second arch in 1831.

Although the bridge had been repaired, the foundations had become unsafe. A project to replace it was started in the 1860s with a new bridge designed with three main cast-iron arch spans, each 100 feet braced by wrought iron girders made by the Derby iron-maker, Andrew Handyside.

Planned by the borough surveyor, M. O. Tarbotton, the width between the parapets was 40 feet – widened to 80 feet in 1924/26. The general contractor was Benton and Woodiwiss of Derby and construction started in 1868. It was completed in 1871 at a cost of £30,000 – the equivalent of around 2.5 million pounds today. The two bridges stood side by side for a time, the old bridge being demolished on 18 October 1872 and the new bridge opened on 25 July 1871. Two arches, which are to be seen in the middle of the traffic island at the south end of Trent Bridge, are left to remind us of this old bridge.

On the northern abutment of the bridge, the high-water marks reached by floods since 1852 have been carved into the stonework. This practice was started during the period when the Heth Beth bridge still existed, and those earlier marks were transferred onto the new bridge. To enable a comparison to be made with the peak levels, a graduated series of heights in feet above sea level has also been added. The highest flood mark is attributed to the 1795 flood, with a height at the bridge of 24.55 m. Normal water level, which is controlled by Holmes Sluices 4 km downstream, is 20.7 m.

The new Trent Bridge formed part of a series of works along the banks of the river to improve flood defences, and constructed the stepped, stone embankments known as the Victoria embankment. People came here to promenade or sit on the embankment steps that make a perfect grandstand for watching events on the river. Pleasure boats sailed from here to Wilford and Colwick Park where entertainment and refreshment was provided. The memorial gardens on the Victoria Embankment were a gift of Jesse Boot who made the announcement of his offer in his acceptance speech when he received the Freedom of the city of Nottingham in 1920. The statue of Queen Victoria was removed from the Market Square to the Victoria Embankment, beside Trent Bridge in 1953.

A new bridge across the Trent to relieve the congestion on Trent Bridge was officially opened by Princess Alexandra of Kent on 5 June 1958. Clifton Bridge is 795 feet long with a central span of 275 feet. At the time, this was the longest span of pre-stressed concrete in Britain.

Trent Bridge Inn

The early Trent Bridge Inn was located just outside the walls of the city of Nottingham where travellers could stay while they waited to enter the city the following morning. It was owned by the Musters family of Colwick Hall who owned land in West Bridgford, but the inn's main claim to fame is the fact that it was instrumental in creating the world famous Trent Bridge cricket ground.

Cricket at Trent Bridge

The first reference to cricket is dated 1344 when it was known as club ball. The word cricket did not appear until 1598 and the first rules of the game were not published until 1744. There were only two stumps 22 inches high, and the bails were 6 inches long until a third was added in 1777. The earliest known reference to cricket being

Trent Bridge Inn (Old), Nottingham.

An early photograph of the Trent Bridge Inn.

played in Nottingham was the Nottingham Cricket Club *v.* Sheffield Cricket Club match on the Forest Racecourse on the 26 and 27 August 1771. The outcome of the game was not determined because of a dispute among the players, but this inter-county match was a significant milestone.

William Clarke, who was born in 1798, was the captain of the Nottinghamshire cricket team, but he was a bricklayer by trade. In 1812, he gave this up to become landlord of the Bell Inn, before marrying Mary Chapman, the landlady of the Trent Bridge Inn, and moving there. Clarke had a vision – a cricket team in competition to the one owned by the town council. The Clarke's arranged for the land behind the inn to be made available and had it cleared and fenced so that cricket matches could be held here in preference to the former location within the city. The site had the added advantage of the inn, where players could take refreshment or rest during the matches.

The first match was in 1835. Although he persevered, the cricket matches did not attract large crowds and he was forced to experiment with other attractions. In 1845, Clarke decided to move to London and founded the All England Eleven, which became a nationally known touring cricket team. Clarke died in 1856 and John Chapman, who was Clarke's stepson, took over the management of the inn and ground, but he and his successors enjoyed no great success. Richard Daft, who was a well-known cricketer at Trent Bridge, ran the inn at one time and captained the club for ten years, but he died bankrupt in 1900. At the end of the First World War, the Musters family sold the inn and the ground to the cricket club. The club only briefly owned the inn as they resold it to a brewery and gave them the right to supply food to the ground in perpetuity.

Today, Trent Bridge is one of Nottingham's most famous landmarks and is synonymous with one of England's biggest and most famous cricket grounds. Nottinghamshire County Cricket Club is one of the eighteen major county clubs that make up the English and Welsh domestic cricket structure.

Road Transport

The making and repair of roads had always been the responsibility of the Lords of the Manor until the mid-sixteenth century when it became the responsibility of the parish. The crude methods of construction and repair became inadequate as wheeled carts and wagons replaced packhorses and roads deteriorated further under the heavier use. In the mid-seventeenth century, a new concept of turnpiking was introduced whereby the cost of construction and maintaining the highways came from road users who had to pay at various stages along the route. By the end of 1750, 146 turnpike trusts had been formed, managing around 3,400 miles of highway. Over the next twenty-two years, a further 418 trusts were formed improving highways and travel.

In 1770, the Nottingham to London stagecoach left Nottingham at 5 a.m. on Tuesdays. Passengers slept at Northampton and arrived in the metropolis at 7 p.m. on Thursday evening. The first mail coaches ran between Nottingham and London in 1784. They left London at 6 p.m. reaching Nottingham at 6 a.m. the following day. In 1797, Joseph Raynor was the postmaster and his duty was to go round the town morning and evening ringing his bell. If you had a letter or parcel to post, or were expecting one, you listened for his bell and approached him.

The Nottingham Canal

This was a great time for the establishment of new industries, but expansion was often hampered by poor transportation links and increasingly inadequate roads. Stimulated by the vastly increased industrial production, canal mania hit Britain in 1757 when businessmen recognised the potential in this improved means of conveying goods.

The idea for the Nottingham canal was first raised in 1790 and passed through Parliament in 1791. The canal, which was 23.6 km long, began at the Cromford Canal, just north of its junction with the Erewash Canal at Langley Mill, proceeds to the Trent at Nottingham with a branch to the river at Lenton.

During the winter of 1794/95, severe frosts were followed by floods, which caused a great deal of damage. But despite the problems the canal, opened in 1796 having cost twice the initial estimate of £43,500. At first, the canal was praised by the citizenry who saw shipments of building materials, coal and agricultural tools come into the area. However, the canal owners' tolls soon became excessive and led to mass discontent. When the first railways arrived in the 1840s, a number of shippers quickly abandoned the canals. Throughout the nineteenth century, the Nottingham canal was in continuous decline as a transport route, and it was finally abandoned altogether in 1936. The following year, the London & North Eastern Railway that owned it shut down the main stretch of the canal.

Although abandoned, the canal still caused problems. In times of heavy rainfall, it flooded surrounding areas of the city, so Nottingham City Council bought the section running through the city, and from 1955 a programme of filling in the canal began. Most of the route was subsequently built over. The section from Derby Road to Lenton Chain was reused as a new course for the River Leen, so is still in water, and the northern section is a local nature reserve.

Canal Street, previously called Leen Side, was dominated by Victorian buildings and the British Waterways building, originally the Trent Navigation warehouse. Fronting the street was the aptly named pub, the Narrow Boat, which closed in 1996 – a reminder of the heyday of the country's canals. Now the area has been transformed, the canal is used for leisure and the buildings converted into bars and restaurants.

Nottingham canal in the nineteenth century.

Nottingham Public Transport

Plans for a tramway in the town of Nottingham started as early as 1870, and sufficient progress was made by a syndicate of local businessmen to formally establish a tramways company. In January 1872, the Nottingham Tramways applied for a provisional order authorising them to construct and operate tramways in Nottingham. The initial suggestion was deemed too ambitious and a scaled down submission dealing with two lines only was successful. In 1875, the company name was changed to the Nottingham and District Tramways Co. Ltd, then the Nottingham Corporation Tramways when it was taken over by the Nottingham Corporation. The order authorised the company to operate from 1877 by animal power only. It was on 17 September 1878 that the first two sections of the authorised tramway were opened. One line ran from St Peter's Square and Trent Bridge via Albert Street, Lister Gate, Carrington Street and Arkright Street, and to the east end of Station Street; the other ran from the junction of Station Street and Carrington Street along Arkwright Street to the Union Inn on London Road.

The trams ran on rails weighing around 45lbs per yard and were double-headed with a groove, bolted to a wrought-iron plate about a foot wide; each rail was 27 feet long.

Two years later another section was opened from the Market Place via Chapel Bar, Derby Road, Alfreton Road, Radford Road to Church Street, Basford. On the outward journey, this route needed two extra horses up the long Derby Hill Road. Passengers paid 2d to ascend the hill, 1d to ride down. On 1 December 1879, the company was operating 20 cars, using 192 horses. They were carrying an average of 55,000 passengers per week. The following two years saw the opening of two further routes from the Market Place to Carrington where a depot and stable were established the whole length of Forest Road connecting the Carrington and Basford routes, which completed the construction and operation of all routes authorised by the 1877 Act.

With the use of mechanical power permitted under the 1884 Act, a steam train operated for a little while on the Basford route, but the horse-drawn tram regained the route very quickly. In 1897, the town council decided to buy the tramway for £80,000. Six months later they gained approval for a reconstruction and expansion

The first public horse-drawn tram service in Nottingham.

scheme. This included conversion to overhead electric traction on eight routes at an estimated cost of £425,000.

Powers for these were granted in the Nottingham Corporation Act 1899 and electrification began. On 1 January 1901, the first electric tram ran on the Sherwood section, and in May, horse-buses were withdrawn from the St Peter's Square to Musters Road service. In October, the first nine electric trams arrived in Nottingham and were assembled at Sherwood Depot. By November, only one (No. 4) was completed, and this made its trial run on 17 November, loaded with 3 tons of sand to represent the weight of a full load of passengers. The journey into Nottingham was quite successful, but trouble was experienced on its return when climbing Queen Street.

The routes were all either conversions of, or extensions to, horse-tram routes. Horse-buses provided a service connecting with the horse-trams while the old rails were pulled up, but this did not last long. Electric cars superseded the horse-trams on 23 July. Some delay was experienced in obtaining new trams due to the large orders in hand. The service was well patronised, and on Saturdays, all twenty-five tramcars were needed in service, overcrowding being commonplace.

During the next twenty-six years, there were seventeen extensions made to the routes. In 1925, it was time for a change over to trolley or motorbus power. The Nottingham trolleybus system opened on 10 April 1927 and gradually replaced the tramway system. It was completed in 1936, with a total of eight routes and a maximum fleet of 157 trolleybuses. It was closed on 30 June 1966. Between 1932–53, Nottingham was also served by another system, the Nottinghamshire and Derbyshire trolleybus system, which linked the city of Nottingham with Ripley in the neighbouring county of Derbyshire. It opened on 7 January 1932, but the system was a small and short-lived one, with a total of three routes and a maximum fleet of thirty-two trolleybuses. It was closed relatively early on 25 April 1953.

Railway

In terms of railway history, Nottingham was a late starter. A main line bypassed the city until 1836 when the Midland Counties Railway obtained consent to run trains from Rugby via Leicester to Trent, with lines from there to Derby, Nottingham and the Erewash valley. As Nottingham only had branch line status, it was necessary for passengers to go to Derby for through routes. The first station in Nottingham was Nottingham Carrington Street station, opened on 4 June 1839 when the Midland Counties Railway opened the line from Nottingham to Derby. In 1844, the Midland Counties Railway merged with two others into the Midland Railway. By 1848, it had outgrown Carrington Street station and a new through station was opened on Station Road.

The Midland Railway lost its Nottingham monopoly when, in 1893, the Manchester, Sheffield & Lincolnshire Railway obtained authorisation to extend its North Midlands railway network into London. In anticipation of the opening of its London extension, in 1897 it changed its name to the Great Central Railway. It was the last steam mainline in the United Kingdom. It took three years of negotiations to acquire a 13-acre site at a cost of £473,000 in the heart of Nottingham's city centre to build its railway station. The construction called for the demolition of a whole neighbourhood of streets, some

1,300 houses, twenty-four public houses, Nottingham Union Workhouse and St Stephen's church in Bunker Hill. The railway station was being constructed on a grand scale, so the Midland Railway rebuilt the Midland station to compete. On 15 March 1899, the London Extension was officially opened to passenger and freight traffic, allowing more direct journeys from Marylebone in London to Nottingham, Leicester, Sheffield and Manchester.

Nottingham Victoria Railway Station

Both the Great Central Railway and the Great Northern Railway shared the station, but the two owners failed to reach agreement on the station's name. The situation was resolved when the name Nottingham Victoria was chosen, and the planned opening date was to coincide with Queen Victoria's birthday. The main station building was in true Victorian splendour. It was constructed in red brick and Darley Dale stone in Renaissance style, and the three-storey building was dominated by a 100-foot clock tower, topped with a cupola and weather vane. Nottingham Victoria station was officially opened without ceremony by the Nottingham Joint Station Committee in the early hours of 24 May 1900 – over a year after the commencement of services on the new railway line.

The traffic that passed through was very varied and included expresses, local services, cross-country services as well as freight, but by the 1960s locomotives and rolling stock were unreliable and old; the line did not benefit from British Rail's new diesel locomotives. Passenger numbers fell, closure was inevitable and the last through service from Nottingham to London ran on 3 September 1966. Victoria station was finally closed on 4 September 1967 after less than seventy years. The station building was entirely demolished except for the clock tower. The Victoria shopping centre filled the site, incorporating the old station clock tower into the main entrance on Milton Street. It now survives but is dwarfed by the neighbouring block of flats, aptly named Victoria Flats – Nottingham's tallest building at 256 feet tall is here.

Victoria Station, Nottingham.

16

NOTTINGHAM IN THE TWENTIETH CENTURY

Nottingham was an internationally important centre of lace manufacture, but the rapid and poorly planned growth left Nottingham, like many other towns, with slum housing. The population prior to the eighteenth century had been under 4,000, but by 1801 it had risen to 29,000. Forty years later, this figure had doubled and by 1881 it was 159,000. The increase continued in the twentieth century with 240,000 in 1901, rising to 306,000 in 1951.

In the 1920s and 1930s, Nottingham council began building council houses. Many were built on new estates north of the city. None of these developments affected the existing older borough of Nottingham or at least the built up part, which was relatively small until 200 years ago. Between the wars, there was a determined effort to rid the city of its worst dwellings. It's necessary to remove old buildings that have become insanitary and overcrowded, but all too often this wholesale, indiscriminate clearing of an area results in the loss of many fine old buildings too. When the slum properties were cleared from Narrow Marsh in the 1930s, Long Stairs, one of the ancient routes from High Pavement down to Narrow Marsh, was closed as the steps were considered too dangerous. Alongside was Malin Hill, an ancient bridle path from the old town down to the Meadows, and probably the oldest route out of Nottingham to the south. It was named after George Malin who lived there at the beginning of the fourteenth century. The old houses and workshops on the hillside, some of which have two levels of caves below, have been demolished. New buildings have been erected and the Broadmarsh shopping entre was constructed in 1972.

The growing problem of traffic congestion in the centre resulted in a continuous road from Glasshouse Street to London Road now known as Lower Parliament Street, and a new highway known as Maid Marion Way from Parliament Street near Chapel Bar and Park Row through to Castle Boulevard. The demolition of former buildings means that many streets have lost a great deal of character. This has a detrimental effect on an area when historical buildings have been demolished and replaced with anonymous office blocks and shops. After the 1960s, the council's policy changed from wholesale destruction to conservation. Post-war development and the need for more buildings meant that Nottingham was allowed to expand into the fields surrounding the town. In the 1950s and '60s, many more council estates were built in the north of the city. The city of Nottingham is now the seventh largest conurbation in the United Kingdom. It stretches some 9 miles from north to south and 6 miles from east to west.

Nottingham Council House

Nottingham Council House is the city hall of Nottingham, designed by Thomas Cecil Howitt (*see Famous Nottingham Characters*) and built between 1927 and 1929 in the neo-Baroque style. Howitt was in no doubt that the use of classical lines would mean that it would not look dated in a few years' time.

It replaced the former Nottingham Exchange, which had previously stood on the site presiding over the eastern end of the Old Market Square. The foundation stone was laid by Alderman Herbert Bowles, Chairman of the Estates Committee on 17 March 1927, and the building was officially opened by the Prince of Wales (later King Edward VIII) and the Duke of Windsor on 22 May 1929. The total cost of the building at the time was £502,876, – the equivalent of £25.9 million in today's money. By the time the bill was finally cleared in 1981, the total including interest was £620,294.

The Council House and exchange buildings to the rear are constructed of Portland Stone. The terrace overlooking the old market square has eight massive columns. Above

The Old Market Square in the mid-twentieth century with its procession way leading to the impressive Council House.

are twenty-one figures representing the activities of the council. There are sculptured groups and a stone frieze depicting traditional local crafts such as bell founding, mining and alabaster carving. These were designed and created by Joseph Else (1875–1955), principal of the Nottingham School of Art (now part of the Nottingham Trent University), working alongside three extremely gifted former students: James Woodford, Charles L. J Doman, and Ernest Webb. All the sculptors were born and raised in Nottingham. They are also responsible for the famous Art-Deco lions guarding the entrance to the Council House. People arrange to meet at the lions, which are variously called Leo and Oscar, Lennie and Ronnie or Menelaus and Agamemnon. A pub overlooking the square is now named after Joseph Else.

Another striking visual element of the building is the 200-foot-high dome, topped with a golden ball, which is actually made up of sections of gilded lead. It rises above the city skyline, making this an iconic symbol of the city. The dome contains the famous bell, which, being Nottingham is of course named Little John, after Robin Hood's famous sidekick. The bell was cast in 1927 by the world-famous bell founders John Taylor & Co. of Loughborough. The bell and its clock mechanism was manufactured and installed by William W. Cope. Weighing 10 tons, 7 cwt and 27 lb, it's the fifth heaviest bell in the UK and has the deepest tone in the country, the chime of which can be heard for a distance of 7 miles on a still day. With the new look Council House was a new look market square, with raised areas and a processional way. The changes meant the square was no longer able to accommodate a market and events like the Goose Fair had to be moved.

The ground floor of the Council House is predominantly an upmarket, fashion-dominated shopping mall now called the Exchange, although it's often referred to as the Exchange Arcade. Retailing space was included in the design to fund the construction of the building and remained under council control until sold in 1985 and redeveloped as a privately owned shopping centre. Walk between the stylish shops and look up to locate the 28-foot diameter cupola under the dome. In each of the four spandrels you will see impressive frescoes (painting done directly onto plaster) by two local artists, Noel Denholm Davies and Hammersley Ball. Each fresco marks a great event in Nottingham's history. The Danes capturing Nottingham in 868, William the Conqueror ordering the building of the castle in 1068, Robin Hood and His Merry Men and King Charles I raising his standard at the start of the Civil War in 1642.

The artists used local celebrities as models. Thomas Cecil Howitt, the architect responsible for designing the Nottingham Council House, is seen in the guise of William the Conqueror's surveyor. The legendary 6-foot, 4-inch Notts County Goalkeeper, Albert Iremonger, gives his face and physique to Little John, and Mrs Popham, wife of a local doctor, was Maid Marion. The inscription around the base of the dome reads: 'The Corporation of Nottingham erected this building for counsel and welcome, and to show merchandise and crafts.' The upper floors of the Exchange Arcade house council offices.

Damage from the Second World War

Nottingham experienced the Blitz when Germany bombed the city on the evenings of 8 and 9 May, 1941. This was part of a nationwide campaign to disrupt key industrial production, undermine morale and destroy factories, rail networks and infrastructure. During one air raid, 140 people were killed and 4,500 houses destroyed. Large areas of Nottingham and West Bridgeford were flattened. University College on Shakespeare Street, the registry office, the Moot Hall, St John's and St Christopher's churches were amongst the most important buildings destroyed. The May raid was by far the worst air raid on Nottingham, although the city suffered ten other raids, which caused a total of 181 deaths. The buildings on the 13-acre former Boots site, an area that had suffered a lot of war damage, were demolished in 1996 and became the Island Business Quarters. The former Boots printing works and the Nottingham Ice Stadium were demolished to make way for the National Ice Centre, opened in 2000. The complex also houses the Trent FM Arena, which seats 10,000 people for concerts, sporting events, ice shows and exhibitions.

The Change in Use for Nottingham Castle

After the 1831 riots when the castle was gutted, the derelict shell was left for forty-five years as a silent rebuke to the people of Nottingham. The Oxford University Trust bought it from the Duke of Newcastle and it was restored in 1875 by Thomas Chambers Hine. The corporation acquired the lease in 1875 and it was opened by the Prince of Wales (later King Edward VII in 1878) as the first provincial municipal museum of the fine and applied arts. Nottingham Castle became the property of the city in November 1952 when it was purchased from the trust for £16,000. On Christmas Day 1996, a landslide caused by a leaking water main led to 80 tonnes of earth and retaining wall falling to the bottom of the castle rock. This revealed some remains of the original castle foundations and the bedrock. After a lengthy controversy on the best conservation/restoration approach, the terrace was reinstated in 2005 with a traditional stone façade.

The terrace offers great views to the south of the city and appeared in the film *Saturday Night and Sunday Morning* – a groundbreaking film about the changing attitude of youth in a shifting industrial society during the late 1950s (*see Alan Stillicoe in Famous Nottingham Characters*).

A drawing of the Ducal Mansion appeared on millions of packets of rolling tobacco and cigarettes made by John Player & Sons, of Nottingham. Most packets had the phrases 'Nottingham Castle and Trade Mark' bracketing the image of the non-fortress-like structure. Novelist Ian Fleming referred to 'that extraordinary trademark of a dolls house swimming in chocolate fudge with Nottingham Castle written underneath' in *Thunderball*. Written in 1959, it was the ninth book in the James Bond series where Bond is the secret service operator 007. Fleming's British readers at the time would have been familiar with the image of Nottingham Castle associated with their cigarettes.

The ducal mansion is still in use as a museum and art gallery. It houses most of the City of Nottingham's fine and decorative art collections, galleries on the history and archaeology of Nottingham and the surrounding areas, and the regimental museum of the Shewood Foresters. Nottingham Castle now plays host to a number of public annual events. These include the Nottingham Beer Festival and the Robin Hood

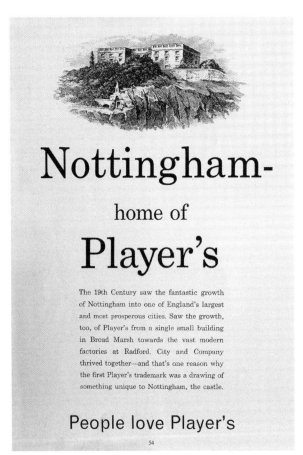

Player's advert was so familiar that Ian Fleming referred to it in his novel *Thunderball*.

Pageant. In 2008, when 1,119 people arrived at the castle dressed as Robin Hood, it was a world record. Three years later, the record was broken by 1,215 people dressed as Robin Hood assembling at Newark showground, which shows that the popularity of our local hero continues indefinitely.

A New Look for the Old Market Square

The Old Market Square is the now the largest surviving square in the United Kingdom, covering an area of approximately 22,000 m². It has been at the centre of Nottingham life for over 1,000 years, but the new millennium meant a new look for Nottingham's Old Market Square. Eighty years after it had been laid out with several platforms creating a central procession way in 1927, the decline in the quality, changes in function and issues surrounding disabled access meant changes were again necessary. Redesigned by Gustafson Porter in 2004 and completed in March 2007, the Old Market Square was built using three shades of granite. The central open space is a single tier and includes the recreation of an ancient border that once divided Nottingham.

Historically, the square forms a meeting place for the people of Nottingham and is also the location for local events, civic protests, royal visits, celebrations and public mourning. A number of Nottingham's defining moments have taken place in the square. Trophies won by Nottingham Forest Football Club, including the European Cup and the FA Cup, have all been held aloft in front of crowds here. Nottingham ice dance legends Torvill and Dean (*see Famous Nottingham Characters*) stood on the Council House balcony overlooking the Market Square following their famous Olympic triumph.

In 2004, a memorial service to remember the life of Nottingham Forest's former manager, Brian Clough OBE, was held there in front of national television cameras and thousands of local football supporters in the square. Brian Clough was regarded by many football fans as the greatest manager in the history of English football. His career at Nottingham Forest spanned the duration of 1975–93, and now his statue stands just off the square at the junction of King and Queen Street.

17

FAMOUS NOTTINGHAM CHARACTERS

William Booth

William Booth was born on 10 April 1829, the second son of five children born to Samuel Booth and his second wife, Mary Moss. Thirteen-year-old William was apprenticed to a pawnbroker and, two years into his apprenticeship, he was converted to Methodism and became a Methodist lay preacher. When his apprenticeship ended in 1848, he was unemployed and spent a year looking in vain for work. In 1849, he reluctantly left Nottingham and moved to London, where he again found work with a pawnbroker. Booth tried to continue lay preaching in London, and began open-air evangelising in the streets and on Kennington Common.

In 1851, Booth joined the Methods Reform Church, and on 10 April 1852 his twenty-third birthday, he left pawn broking and became a full-time preacher at their

William Booth, founder of the Salvation Army.

headquarters at Binfield chapel in Clapham. In 1855, he married Catherine Mumford from Ashbourne, Derbyshire, and together they founded the Christian mission, which was to spread over Britain. Having organised their followers on military lines, in 1878, the Mission became known as the Salvation Army. William Booth was honoured by the heads of many countries, and in 1905 his native town of Nottingham made him an Honorary Freeman – the first person to be honoured in this way.

He died on 20 August 1912. The row of terraced house on Notintone Place where he was born was bought by the Salvation Army in the 1930s. Part was demolished and the remainder turned into an Eventide Home and Goodwill Centre with museum, which opened in 1971. The statue of General Booth, a copy of the original stands at the Salvation Army's training college in Denmark Hill, London, was unveiled by his granddaughter, Commissioner Catherine Bramwell-Booth, at the opening of the complex.

William Abednego Thompson, Bare-knuckle Boxing Champion of England

In the slums of Nottingham in 1811, a miner's wife living at No. 20 New Yard, now Trinity Walk, gave birth to triplets. She named them Shadrach, Meshach and Abednego, from the book of Daniel in the Bible. The births are registered in St Mary's church as the last of twenty-one children born into the family. From an early age, Abednego was noted for his sporting ability. When he was fifteen his father died and Abednego was sent to the Nottingham workhouse with his mother. At the first opportunity he left there and sold oysters in and around the streets of Nottingham before obtaining a job as an iron turner. By the age of eighteen, he was already fighting for money to provide for his family. At the age of twenty-one, he was a regular bare- knuckle prize fighter tutored by the English champion of the time, Jem Wood. He was also very agile, earning the name Bendy because of his constant bobbing and weaving around the ring. His nickname evolved and Bendy Abednego became Bendigo. His speed and agility won him his fights, but it was Bendigo's personality and sense of humour that endeared him to the crowd. Soon he was drawing crowds of over 10,000 people to his illicit fights, held secretly out of town in barns or fields.

A crowd favourite, in 1839, when he was twenty-eight, he went for the 'All England' title and gained it in front of a crowd of 15,000 people. William Abednego Thompson, nicknamed the Nottingham Jester, was Champion Prize Fighter of All England. A public house in Sneinton, Nottingham, was named the Old Wrestlers pub after its famous resident. It was converted to Bendigo's in 1957. Rather ironically, it was forced to close in the late 1990s due to the fighting and brawling.

Richard Bonington – Artist

Richard Parkes Bonington was born at what is now Bonington House, High Street, Arnold, in October 1802. He moved with his family to France in 1817 and studied art at an advanced level. Inspired by the old masters, his work as a romantic landscape painter was much in demand and he painted with feverish energy. He exhibited at the Royal Academy of Art in 1827 and 1828, but, on 23 September 1828, aged only twenty-six, he died of TB. The Bonington Theatre, the local junior school, Bonington

Drive and Bonington Street all get their names from him. His bust is on display in Bonington theatre, there is a statue in the Gedling Borough Council Offices in Arnold, two of his pictures hang in Nottingham Castle Museum, and the art gallery in the centre of Nottingham also bears his name.

Thomas Cecil Howitt OBE – Architect

Thomas Cecil Howitt was the architect responsible for designing the Nottingham Council House that stands at the head of the Old Market Square. He was born on 6 June 1889 at Hucknall, educated at Nottingham High School, leaving in 1904 to be apprenticed to the prominent Nottingham architect, Albert Nelson Bromley. He studied briefly at the Architectural Association School in London, and later opened a London branch office for Bromley before returning to the Nottingham office. Following a study tour of Europe in early 1914, Howitt was invited to become the company architect for Boots. However, the war soon intervened. He was commissioned in November 1914, rising to the rank of Lieutenant Colonel in the Leicester Regiment. He was awarded the DSO (Distinguished Service Order) and a Chevalier of the Legion d'Honneur for action at the Battle of the Marne. Howitt was demobilised with the rank of major in October 1919, and joined the City Engineer's Department at Nottingham City Council. He was housing architect for the city council, designing municipal housing estates, which are often considered to be among the finest in terms of planning in the country

In 1926, Howitt was elected as a member of the RIBA Council as work on the Nottingham Council House began. That completed, he set up his own practice and established an office in exchange buildings in December 1930. He designed many civic buildings throughout the country, but his chief architectural legacies are in his home city of Nottingham. He was actively involved in RIBA matters during the 1950s and finally retired in April 1962. He died aged seventy-nine in September 1968, in the house he designed for himself in the village of Orston, Nottinghamshire.

James Arthur Woodford RA OBE – Sculptor

James Arthur Woodford was born at No. 38 Alfreton Street, Nottingham, on 25 November 1893. His father, Samuel Woodford, was a lace designer who passed his artistic talent to his remarkably gifted son, who became one of the finest sculptors of the twentieth century. During the First World War, James served with the 11th Battalion Nottinghamshire and Derbyshire Regiment, Sherwood Foresters, and was mentioned in despatches. His studies had been disrupted by the war, but when that ended he returned to the Nottingham School of Art and the Royal College of Art. In September 1920/21, he was listed as a student aged twenty-five, living at No. 38 Alfred Street, Nottingham. He was awarded the Prix de Rome for sculpture in 1922, elected to the Royal Academy in 1945 and nominated by Joseph Else, principal of Nottingham School of Art, as a fellow of the Royal Society of British Sculptors.

When Thomas Howitt designed Nottingham's neoclassical Council House (1927–29), Joseph Else and three former students of the School of Art – Charles L. J Doman, James Woodford and Ernest Webb – were responsible for the impressive statuary around the building. All the sculptors were born and raised in Nottingham. James Woodford sculpted the group called Prosperity at the Long Row East corner, best seen from outside the Yorkshire Bank. Not only was he an extremely gifted sculptor, he was also a painter and engraver working in many mediums and with many materials including bronze, clay, plaster, stone and wood. Other early work included three sets of bronze doors with relief panels for Norwich City Hall. Each of these remarkable doors has three relief roundels showing Norwich's manual trades. In 1939, Woodford produced the stone figures and panels for Huddersfield Library and Art Gallery, and the sculptures on either side of the main entrance. During the Second World War, James Woodford was a camouflage officer with the Air Ministry. After the war, he was commissioned to carve the war memorial of the British Medical Association for the central courtyard of its headquarters in Tavistock Square, London. This work produced in 1954 was to form a memorial to the medical men and women who died in the Second World War. Designed by James Woodford, it consists of a bronze fountain in the form of the staff of Asclepius, the Greek god of healing, surrounded by four allegorical figures in Portland stone representing sacrifice, cure, prevention and aspiration.

He produced bronze doors, stone pylon figures and plaster ceiling panels for the Royal Institute of British Architects (RIBA) building in Portland Place, London. The themed bronze doors are quite spectacular. Each measures 12 feet by 6 feet and weigh 1 ½ tons. They depict the London scene represented by places like London Zoo, and a London Underground tube tunnel. He also had commissions for the liner *Queen Mary*, panels for St John's Wood Barracks, various keystones for the DEFRA building in Whitehall, carved timber screens in the chancel of St Thomas the Apostle church on the Boston Road, Hanwell, Middlesex, decorated with angels each playing a different instrument.

Back in Nottingham, to commemorate the city's quincentenary in 1949, James Woodward was asked to produce something unique to Nottingham. His Robin Hood memorial is an unusual arrangement of four free-standing figures dominated by a 7-foot statue of Robin Hood and wall reliefs in bronze. It was presented to the city by Philip Clay, a local businessman, and stands on the terrace below the outer walls of Nottingham Castle.

In an interview for the 'Home Chat' section of *Picture Post*, James Woodford related that as a schoolboy, he would watch the Sherwood Foresters drilling in front of Nottingham Castle just where his Robin Hood statue and side bronzes now stand. Little did he realise that he would serve with the Sherwood Foresters in the First World War, or that he would be commissioned to sculpt the statues that now stand there.

James Woodford was awarded the OBE in 1953. Apart from his public sculptural and ecclesiastical work, he did a considerable amount of work in the heraldic field. For the Queen's Coronation in 1953, he was commissioned by the Ministry of Public Buildings and Works to model a series of ten heraldic beasts to stand at the entrance to Westminster Abbey for the occasion. On 6 February 1953, the *Evening Standard* featured an article on the sculptures and two photographs – one of Woodford at work on *The Lion of England* at his Chiswick studio, and the other of Woodford showing the then Minister of Works, Mr David Eccles, a scale model. The heraldic beasts include the *Black Bull of Clarence*, the *Falcon of the Plantaganets*, the *Griffin of Edward III*, the *Red Lion of England*, the *Red Dragon of Wales*, the *Unicorn of*

Scotland, The *White Greyhound of Richmond*, the *White Horse of Hanover*, the *White Lion of Mortimer* and the *Yale of Beaufort*. James Woodford told the reporter that 5 tons of clay was used to sculpt the ten heraldic beasts, which were then produced using 2 tons of plaster. Obviously the plaster originals were not intended to be permanent. However, thanks to funding by an anonymous donor, replicas of these ten figures were carved by James Woodford from Portland Stone and are now in The Royal Botanical Gardens in Kew. James Arthur Woodford RA OBE died on 8 November 1976, aged eighty-five.

Nottingham's Three Rebel Writers

Lord George Byron – Freedom Fighter and One of England's Greatest Poets

Born in London in 1788, George Gordon Byron was the son of Capt. John Byron and Catherine Gordon, originally a rich woman whose fortune had been squandered by her husband. George Gordon was ten when he succeeded the title 6th Baron Byron of Rochdale and inherited the family seat Newstead abbey from his uncle. It's believed to have been one of the religious houses established by Henry II around 1170 in expiation of the murder of Archbishop Thomas Becket. After the Dissolution in 1539, the buildings came into the hands of the Byron family who were created Barons of Rochdale in 1643.

Befitting his position, George Gordon Byron was educated at Harrow School and Trinity College, Cambridge. His first collection of poems, *Hours of Idleness*, appeared in 1807, and in 1809 Byron set off on his grand tour where he visited Spain, Malta, Albania and Greece. His poetical account of this grand tour, *Childe Harold's Pilgrimage* published in 1812, established Byron as one of England's leading poets.

After winning early fame as the most fashionable poet of Georgian England, Byron's reputation turned from celebrity to notoriety. He scandalized London society by starting an affair with Lady Caroline Lamb, wife of Queen Victoria's prime minster, Lord Melbourne, and was ostracized when he was suspected of having a sexual relationship with his half-sister, Augusta Leigh, who gave birth to an illegitimate daughter.

In 1811, in his maiden speech in the House of Lords, he defended the actions of the Luddites and the spoke against the Frame Breaking Bill, by which the government intended to apply the death penalty to Luddites. He became a strong advocate of social reform and used his poems to put over his political views. In 1815, Byron married Anne Isabella Milbanke, but the relationship came to an end the following year. Exiled by hostile public opinion, amid mounting debts and the aftermath of a disastrous marriage, in 1817, he was forced to sell Newstead abbey – run down by the excesses of the 5th Lord Byron.

George Gordon Byron travelled extensively through Europe and the near East, at the same time writing some of his best work. He supported attempts by the Greek people to free themselves from Turkish rule. In 1823, he joined the Greek insurgents who had risen against the Turks, but in April 1824 he died of marsh fever in Missolonghi.

D. H. Lawrence – the Greatest Imaginitive Novelist of his Generation

David Herbert Lawrence was the fourth child of Lydia Beardsall, a former pupil teacher from Sneinton, and Arthur Lawrence, a barely literate Nottinghamshire coalminer. The family lived in the small mining community of Eastwood, and owing to her family's financial difficulties Lydia had to do manual work in a lace factory. Determined that her son would never be a coalminer, she taught him well and he became the first local pupil to win a county council scholarship to Nottingham High School. He left in 1901, and from 1902 to 1906 David Lawrence served as a pupil teacher at the British School, Eastwood. He went on to become a full-time student and received a teaching certificate from University College, Nottingham, in 1908. During these early years he was working on his first poems, some short stories and a draft of a novel, which eventually become *The White Peacock*. At the end of 1907, he won a short story competition in the *Nottingham Guardian*, the first time that he had gained any wider recognition for his literary talents.

In the autumn of 1908, the newly qualified Lawrence left his childhood home for London. He continued writing, and some of his early poetry, came to the attention of the editor of the influential *The English Review* who commissioned the story *Odour of Chrysanthemums*, which was published in that magazine. Heinemann, a London publisher, asked Lawrence for more work and his career as a professional author began in earnest, although he taught for another year. His first published novel, *The White Peacock*, appeared in 1910 with settings that were heavily inspired by the local Nottinghamshire countryside. His autobiographical novel *Sons and Lovers* is a work that draws upon much of the writer's provincial upbringing. He travelled widely in Europe, Mexico and Australia, but retained a deep feeling for his native Nottinghamshire, which he referred to as 'the country of my heart'.

His style, language and frank treatment of subjects such as female sexuality changed the face of English literature and can still court controversy today. *Lady Chatterley's Lover* became the centre of a famous indecency trial, marking an important transition in public views on censorship and the arts. Lawrence's opinions earned him many enemies and he endured official persecution, censorship, and misrepresentation of his creative work, but E. M. Forster described him as the 'greatest imaginative novelist' of our generation.

Allan Sillitoe – Writer for the Oppressed Workers

Alan Sillitoe was born in Nottingham on 4 March 1928 to poor working-class parents, Christopher Sillitoe and Sabina (*née* Burton). His father was an illiterate, violent tannery worker often unemployed. Alan's childhood was shadowed by the financial problems of the family, who were often on the brink of starvation. He left school at the age of fourteen and worked at the Raleigh Bicycle Factory for the next four years, spending his free time reading prodigiously and being a 'serial lover of local girls'. He then joined the Royal Air Force, but returning from Malaya he was discovered to have tuberculosis and spent sixteen months in an RAF hospital to be pensioned off at twenty-one on 45s a week.

He lived in France and Spain for seven years in an attempt to recover, spending his time writing. In 1955, he was working on his best known piece *Saturday Night and Sunday*

Morning, strongly influenced by his own experiences and the disillusionment of post-war Britain. Arthur Seaton, the anti-hero of his novel, has a dead-end job at a local factory and bemoans the lack of opportunities for the working class and the inevitable end of his youthful philandering. Published in 1958, it was adapted as a film in 1960 with Albert Finney as Arthur Seaton, the young factory worker. Filming took place in and around Nottingham and in particular at the Raleigh factory, where Sillitoe had worked and the Eight Bells public house on St Peter's Gate shortly after its closure in 1959.

Sillitoe wrote around thirty novels and several volumes of poetry. In the 1960s, he was celebrated in the Soviet Union as a spokesman for the oppressed workers in the West, and invited to tour the country several times. In 1990, he was awarded an honorary degree from Nottingham Trent University and the University of Nottingham awarded him an honorary D. Litt in 1994. His 1995 autobiography *Life Without Armour* was critically acclaimed. He was elected a Fellow of the Royal Society of Literature in 1997. In June 2008 he was made an Honorary Freeman of the City of Nottingham – the thirty-fifth person to be given this honour. He died on 25 April 2010 aged eighty-two.

Jayne Torvill and Christopher Dean

Jayne Torvill and Christopher Dean were both born in Nottingham in 1957 and 1958 respectively. Having developed a love of ice skating at a young age, the pair started ice dancing competitively with other partners in the early 1970s and danced together for the first time in 1975. Successful placing in European and World Championships between 1978 and 1980 lead to Chris and Jayne becoming British National Dance Champions in 1980. In 1981, the duo won the European Championships and the World Championships for the first time. They were awarded the MBE (Members of the Order of the British Empire) and were named in the 1981 Queen's Birthday Honours List for their services to ice skating. By 1984, they had achieved first place in the World Championships for the fourth time.

The couple's defining moment was winning gold with their interpretation of Ravel's 'Bolero' at the 1984 Olympics in Sarajevo. In November 1983, the routine had been debuted at the British Championships in Nottingham. Bolero was a masterpiece, taking ice dancing to a completely new level, earning them an unprecedented maximum score and an Olympic gold medal. Twenty-four million viewers were glued to their televisions, captivated by such a great British sporting triumph. Torvill and Dean won the BBC Sports Personality of the Year award in 1984 – the only time it has been awarded jointly to more than one person. In between tours, they won the gold medal in the 1994 European championships and a bronze at that years' Olympics. They announced their retirement in 1998 and were honoured with an OBE (Officers of the Order of British Empire) in the 2000 Queen's Millennium Honours List for their services to ice skating. They were enticed out of retirement to take part in ITV's *Dancing on Ice* and its Australian version, *Torvill and Dean's Dancing on Ice*.

Nottingham is not just the childhood home of Jayne Torvill and Christopher Dean, it is the home of the National Ice Centre where this famous couple lead the first public skating session. The square in front of the building was renamed 'Bolero Square' to honour their great achievements.